TEAM BUILDING
THROUGH
PHYSICAL
CHALLENGES

Donald R. Glover, MEd
White Bear Lake Area Public Schools, Minnesota

Daniel W. Midura, MEd
Roseville Area Schools, Minnesota

Human Kinetics Publishers

Library of Congress Cataloging-in-Publication Data

Glover, Donald R.
    Team building through physical challenges / Donald R. Glover,
Daniel W. Midura.
        p.   cm.
    ISBN 0-87322-359-4
    1. Teamwork (Sports).   2. Physical education and training--Study
and teaching.   I. Midura, Daniel W., 1948-   . II. Title.
    GV706.8.G58 1992   92-2936
    796'.01--dc20   CIP

ISBN: 0-87322-359-4

Acquisitions Editor: Rick Frey, PhD; **Developmental Editor:** Mary E. Fowler;
Assistant Editors: Valerie Hall, Moyra Knight, and Dawn Roselund; **Copyeditor:**
Merv D. Hendricks; **Proofreaders:** Kathy Bennett and Dawn Barker; **Produc-
tion Director:** Ernie Noa; **Typesetter:** Julie Overholt; **Text Design:** Keith
Blomberg; **Text Layout:** Denise Peters and Denise Lowry; **Cover Design:** Jack
Davis; **Cover Photo:** Lorri Bettenga; **Interior Art:** Gretchen Walters, Cindy
Butler, and Lorri Bettenga; **Printer:** Versa Press

Some epigraphs from "The Edge—The Guide to Fulfilling Dreams, Maximizing
Success and Enjoying a Lifetime of Achievement," by Howard E. Ferguson,
Getting the Edge Company, 1990.

Printed in the United States of America   10 9 8 7 6 5 4 3

Human Kinetics Books
A Division of Human Kinetics
P.O. Box 5076, Champaign, IL 61825-5076
1-800-747-4457

Canada: Human Kinetics, Box 24040, Windsor, ON N8Y 4Y9
1-800-465-7301 (in Canada only)

Europe: Human Kinetics, P.O. Box IW14, Leeds LS16 6TR, England
0532-781708

Australia: Human Kinetics, P.O. Box 80, Kingswood 5062, South Australia
618-374-0433

New Zealand: Human Kinetics, P.O. Box 105-231, Auckland 1
(09) 309-2259

To our sons, Luke and Seth Midura and Matt Glover, as they enter their ''team-building'' years.

Contents

Preface

Our country is built upon the concept of teamwork—the kind of teamwork that promotes cooperation and cohesiveness over competition, teamwork in which everyone contributes a part to make a stronger whole. Each "team" in our society, whether it be a sales force, a manufacturing group, a sports team, or a family, must work together for our society to flourish and operate smoothly.

When an organization has a goal, the members mobilize, enthusiasm builds, and excitement grows as the group moves toward success. Every member on a successful team wants to play a part, because each is concerned with the outcome of the group's efforts. Sometimes a team falls short of its goal. Indeed a team might break down if its members do not know how to organize, interact, and plan for progress. But the excitement, the enthusiasm, the concern for the group's progress are what help us learn about accomplishing goals. Even if a group falls short of its target, each wins in learning about becoming a team. Individuals achieve simply by experiencing the process of team building. This process of working cooperatively rather than competitively is what this book is about.

We believe physical education lends itself particularly well to developing cooperative learning. Though physical education is primarily concerned with physical fitness and skills, its focus is expanding to include activities that promote social, psychological, and personal development. We as physical educators have an exciting opportunity to learn strategies to capitalize on this expanding curriculum. We have always talked about teaching teamwork values through sports, but not all students have been able to share in those lessons. Now we know how to make everyone who participates a contributing, enthusiastic, compliment-giving, and compliment-getting part of a team working together toward achieving goals. *Team building* is the name of the concept. Using what we call *physical challenges* is how we teach it.

Team Building Through Physical Challenges gives teachers, recreational supervisors, coaches, and anyone who is in a team-building capacity concrete activities that promote teamwork and enhance the social skills of every participant. Team builders and teammates will learn to work together, have fun together, and accomplish goals together.

The challenges in this book require participants to interact with others, so that even the most reserved person becomes an important part of the group.

Team members need to listen to others, praise them for their ideas, and encourage them in their efforts. These skills of listening, praising, and encouraging are ones that many teachers, coaches, parents, and recreational leaders need to develop, and they can be learned at any age.

This book describes 22 team challenges you can use. All of the challenges are physical, yet all provide opportunities for learners to develop specific skills in communication, decision making, conflict resolution, risk taking, and affirmation. You will learn how to conduct physical challenges through detailed descriptions and multiple possible solutions.

Team building through physical challenges gives each teammate the joy of individual success, but more importantly reinforces the joy of the group accomplishing a task by helping and depending upon one another. These team-building activities, with minor modifications for age, are ideal for children in 1st through 12th grades. The ideas contained in this book can help coaches build closer relationships among team members.

We have used team-building activities for more than 15 years and find that our students enthusiastically look forward to participating.

Team building through physical challenges will change your approach to teaching. Try these challenges and you and your "teammates" will achieve more physically and improve your self-images.

Acknowledgments

The authors wish to thank Laurel Sulack for her word-processing work and Lorri Bettenga for the photography that appears in this book. Our thanks also go to Donna Fuller for her encouragement, and to Mary Fowler for her editorial guidance.

Chapter 1

Developing Teamwork

It's amazing how much can be accomplished
if you don't care who gets the credit.

Blanton Collier
Former NFL coach

Cooperation and teamwork: skills for the present and the future.

Why Develop Teamwork?

Do you remember being on a team that was a winner? Perhaps you were on a basketball team that won a championship. Maybe your business firm closed a big deal, or you were in a hiking group that reached its challenging destination. If you have had that experience of success, wouldn't you like it again? Didn't that winning feeling boost your self-confidence? We all would like to capture that sense of achievement again and again.

Working together in accomplishing goals provides group members with excitement and feelings of success.

Building a Positive Self-Concept

Success depends on a lot of factors, with a primary one being self-concept. Self-concept is largely developed by how others perceive us and react to our efforts. If we receive positive reactions and our social development flourishes, then we have a better chance to succeed.

Self-confidence grows as physical challenges are successfully mastered. As we gain self-confidence and succeed at progressively harder challenges, we feel better about ourselves and our abilities. With a positive self-concept, one can overcome failures and eventually gain success. A positive self-concept gives a person courage to try.

Physical challenges offer a process that builds self-confidence both for individuals and groups. When a person's effort helps a group accomplish its goal, that person is accepted as an integral part of a winning team. As the concept of belonging to a successful team develops, each person takes an active role, rather than being a passive observer.

Team building breeds success without any losers, as happens in a competition. Teammates learn that the cooperative process is what is important—winning becomes a by-product.

Learning Different Roles

Leaders and followers always emerge when people work together as a team, yet everyone in the group will be involved on physical challenge teams. Students who have had great success in traditional physical education settings may find themselves in unfamiliar roles, perhaps dependent on their teammates. Students who have not before enjoyed great success in physical education may discover new motivation and levels of achievement. Students not perceived as physically skilled may become leaders or enjoy new status within the group. Each person is bound to encounter new roles and experiences in team-building activities.

Developing Team Communication

Students will learn that affirmation and cooperation help make any group successful and that being uncooperative divides a group and makes success less likely. For team building to work, everyone must get involved physically and mentally.

Participants in team-building activities soon sense a new atmosphere in the gym. Teammates learn to encourage each other and understand that their success is dependent upon team communication. They will see that the larger the group, the greater the need to communicate—both by talking clearly and listening intently.

Being able to praise a peer is a skill that needs to be learned and reinforced. Accepting praise from teammates also needs to be learned. Exchanging praise helps develop team-building skills and fosters commitment and trust, which are vital to a winning team.

As a team cooperates on physical challenges, all members need to believe their teammates are listening to their ideas. Naturally, some ideas will work, some will be rejected, and some will need to be tested.

When students work together on a challenge, they learn to disagree, to speculate, to take turns, and to diminish tensions. The physical challenges in this book offer students exactly these experiences. Teaching students to be parts of a group and to be good citizens will enhance their self-concepts and will involve them in success experiences.

Success Experiences

A success experience in team building doesn't just mean scoring a touchdown or kicking a goal. A success experience might be contributing an idea and being listened to. We all feel good about ourselves when we can influence the direction of a group. All students in physical education need the opportunity to establish relationships so they feel part of a group. This success experience should permeate physical education and sports. Sometimes only a talented few gain the success experience of recognition for their accomplishments, but everyone involved in team building will attain this reward.

Last, one of the most important success experiences all students have a right to achieve is fun. Students should have fun through play, leave the gym with smiles, and look forward to coming back for more fun.

Decision Making and Learning by Taking Risks

As team members become more relaxed and self-confident, they also become more open to making group decisions rather than having one person decide for them. If team members make successful decisions, individual and team confidence grows, and with it a desire to take intellectual, physical, or emotional risks. Too often teachers, supervisors, and parents are reluctant to allow children to make decisions that affect outcomes and try to protect children from taking risks. We don't want them to fail, yet it is necessary for risk takers and decision makers not only to succeed but, at times, to fail. If we create the right environment, failing in itself can become a path to success. Children will acquire physical, social, and psychological skills necessary for successful living if we allow them to work as a decision-making team that takes risks, makes decisions, succeeds, and, sometimes, fails. The concepts, skills, and dynamics of team building can have far-reaching benefits; team building can prepare children to be confident adults able to make decisions and work well within a group.

When we think of physical education, we usually think of physical fitness and skill development. We agree with the value placed on fitness and skill, but team-building skills create an atmosphere that enhances our ability to meet fitness and skill goals because students, regardless of skill level, will possess increased self-confidence. As students develop more positive interpersonal skills, physical education class becomes a more dynamic environment for all.

Physical challenges can be used at the beginning of a school year, as a specific unit, interspersed between regular curriculum activities, or to culminate your term. Whatever your need, give physical challenges a place in your curriculum and you'll discover great satisfaction in successful team building.

Physical Education's Role in a Child's Development

During the reforms of coming decades, physical education needs to be held as accountable as any other educational subject. Will the reformers consider physical education worthy of mention? We believe that by adding the dimension of team building and the concepts that surround it, we are making physical education more important to a wider variety of people. We believe team building allows each child to contribute to the group and to receive positive recognition for that contribution.

The child who receives positive recognition develops more confidence. As more confidence is developed, the belief in one's abilities is strengthened. The child will accomplish more and perform better in many different endeavors. If students have had the joy of hard work and recognition and of making others happy, they will want that feeling again and again. Children are also great at public relations. If they like something, they let everyone know. As positive recognition and contributing to the group's progress become important and meaningful to children, they will communicate that. Physical education, then, will start to be held in a more positive light in the eyes of parents and other educators.

Society also may ask physical education specialists, "What are you doing to improve our children's fitness?" This demand, considering the decreasing fitness among America's youth, is relevant and important. Physical challenges can help answer that question. By making students part of a successful team and changing their roles from passive to interactive, we can transform negative images about "gym" into positive ones.

Mastering a physical challenge and receiving the accompanying positive feedback from teammates provides students with self-confidence to try a more difficult challenge, to make decisions, and to take risks. We believe increased self-confidence in an atmosphere where students feel good about themselves and their teammates will advance us toward our fitness and skill goals.

Please don't believe that physical challenges create "false" self-confidence. Children know when something is given to them and when something is earned. We all know that when we earn something we take great pride in its ownership. Your team builders should not be allowed to master a challenge until they earn it. Allow failure and struggle. Allow conflict and resolution. Team builders will only improve if they work hard and master a challenge they perceive to be difficult.

Physical educators must be ready to accept responsibility in areas other than skill development in the future. We must contribute to the development of thinking skills and social responsibility. We must win a position of respect alongside other academic offerings. Team building can add to our recognition and respect. Team building is a strategy for the future, and physical educators can be leaders in this concept.

Chapter 2

Warming Up to Team Building

I'm only a reflection of what our team is.

Jim Zorn
Former NFL quarterback

Group support makes the job easier.

Introducing Physical Challenges

When you introduce the physical challenges concept, we suggest you first discuss teamwork. Ask your students what teamwork means or what makes a good team. Someone may suggest that praise is an important part of teamwork. Tell your students that praise raises the confidence of the person being praised and that if they learn to praise teammates, good feelings within the team will result. Why? Because confident teammates try harder.

On pages 9 and 10 you will find the Praise Phrases. Copy and laminate this sheet. Give each student a copy and read through the phrases together. Ask your students if they can suggest other Praise Phrases. Ask the students to practice using the phrases on teammates. Here is a suggested warm-up activity:

Team Workout Warm-Up

Divide into teams of six to eight. Appoint or let the children select one student in each team as organizer. To give everyone a chance, the organizer should vary daily. On signal, organizers run to the instructor, who is at the opposite end of the gym, to receive a list of exercises. The entire team should do these exercises in the order on the card. You may want to vary the order on each card so all the teams are not doing the same order, or you may want to let the team decide the order of the exercises. Here are exercises the team can do together:

- 20 jumping jacks
- 10 push-ups
- Touching opposite sidelines of gym floor 10 times
- 10 sit-ups
- 20 jumps using a jump rope
- Giving the instructor a "high five"
- 10 windmills
- Five coffee grinders
- One team lap around gym
- One high five and one Praise Phrase for everyone in your team upon completion of the exercise card

Some rules we use while the team is doing the warm-up:

1. Team members must wait until all teammates are done before going to the next exercise.
2. The organizer signals when the team can move to the next exercise.
3. Team members huddle to decide which exercise to do next. The huddle gives the team members a feeling of cohesiveness. (The huddle is used only if the instructor has not determined the order of exercises.)
4. Everyone must use at least one Praise Phrase to another teammate or to the team.
5. Teammates should call one another by first names only.

PRAISE PHRASES

Praise and encouragement are two ways we can all feel good about the team. Here are 72 ways to say "Very good!" Copy and laminate this list. Give each student a copy and read through the list together.

1. "Good for you!"
2. "Superb."
3. "You did that very well."
4. "You've got it made."
5. "Terrific!"
6. "Couldn't have done it better myself."
7. "You're doing fine."
8. "You're really improving."
9. "Now you've figured it out."
10. "Outstanding!"
11. "Incredible!"
12. "Good work."
13. "You figured that out fast."
14. "I think you've got it now."
15. "Tremendous!"
16. "You did well today."
17. "Perfect!"
18. "Nice going."
19. "Now you've got the hang of it."
20. "Wow!"
21. "Wonderful!"
22. "You're getting better every day."
23. "You're learning fast."
24. "You make it look easy."
25. "Super!"
26. "You did a lot of work today!"
27. "Keep it up!"
28. "Congratulations."
29. "Exactly right!"
30. "Nice job."
31. "Excellent!"
32. "Sensational!"
33. "You've just about mastered that."
34. "That's really nice."
35. "That's the best ever."
36. "That's great."
37. "Way to go!"
38. "That's the way to do it!"
39. "That's quite an improvement."

40. "Good thinking."
41. "You're really going to town."
42. "Keep up the good work."
43. "That's better."
44. "You nailed that one."
45. "You haven't missed a thing."
46. "Fantastic!"
47. "You're doing a good job."
48. "That's the right way to do it."
49. "Good try."
50. "Right on!"
51. "That's the best you've ever done."
52. "That's RIGHT!"
53. "You must have been practicing!"
54. "Great!"
55. "Keep working on it. You're getting better."
56. "You remembered!"
57. "That kind of work makes me very happy."
58. "You're really working hard today."
59. "I knew you could do it!"
60. "One more time and you'll have it."
61. "Fine!"
62. "That's good."
63. "Good job."
64. "You really make this fun."
65. "Good thinking."
66. "Nothing can stop you now."
67. "You are doing much better today."
68. "Keep on trying."
69. "You are really learning a lot."
70. "You've just about got it."
71. "I've never seen anyone do it better."
72. "You are very good at that."

Can you think of more Praise Phrases? List them here.

73.
74.
75.
76.
77.
78.
79.
80.

Variations

Here are some great alternatives to team workout. One is to use a time limit. Challenge students by asking, "Can your team complete your exercise card in 10 minutes?" Make exercise cards and routines more difficult. Or do the exercises as a relay. The team decides who is going to do which exercise and lines up in relay formation accordingly. One or two members perform the first exercise and tag student Number 2. Continue until all exercises are done. Exercise card relays provide good competition, cooperation, and fitness. Another fun variation also involves a relay. The first person runs to the card pile at the opposite end of the gym. The student reads the card and hands it to the teacher. The student runs back to the team and draws a picture of the exercise, using no letters or numbers and without speaking. After the team guesses the exercise, the artist leads the team in that exercise 15 times. The team continues in relay fashion until everyone has drawn an exercise.

During all variations, the rules apply: Use Praise Phrases; no last names. Remember, the best way to teach is by example, so a high five or pat on the back from you will encourage your students to do the same with their teammates.

Create-A-Game

Create-A-Game is a warm-up that starts group dynamics flowing. The team has to interact by refining skills they have created together. There may be conflict and negative pressure, but students can learn from mistakes. Each team sits in a small circle with equipment such as a ball, three cones, two bowling pins, a rope, and some indoor bases. Add anything else you like. Be creative. Send each team to a separate area of the gym and let it create a game or activity with the equipment.

Watch the interaction. Watch the creativity. Watch the dynamics of the group unfold. As you watch, be more concerned with the *group process* used than with the end product. Give each team 15 minutes to create a game and to practice the skills. After practice, allow each team to show its activity to the others. Then tell the groups the interactions you saw and ask what they noticed. For example, praise a group that seemed to be working together, and point out a group that listened to one another's ideas. Point out negative pressure or put-downs you observed and discuss the influence of this behavior.

Positive Adjectives

After Create-A-Game, have each team sit in a semicircle and give each member a list of positive adjectives to use to describe a personal characteristic of other team members. Samples of such descriptions follow.

POSITIVE ADJECTIVES

Kind	Reserved
Neat	Enthusiastic
Strong	Helpful
Quiet	Aggressive
Nice	Bright
Shy	Thoughtful
Happy	Determined
Active	Convincing
Cheerful	Content
Courteous	Sensible
Intelligent	Creative
Polite	Independent
Friendly	Determined
Energetic	Humorous
Organized	Pleasant
Courageous	Delightful
Honest	Calm
Clever	Confident
Inventive	Daring
Imaginative	

Ask if everyone understands the adjectives. One by one, each team member moves to the front of the team semicircle and faces the teammates as shown in figure 2.1.

Each teammate picks three positive adjectives to describe the teammate in front. The speaker should look at the person in the center, say that person's name, and use the adjectives. For example, "Chris, you are smart, kind, and happy." This may produce giggles at first, but students find that we all enjoy hearing something nice said to us. This exercise gives each teammate an opportunity both to praise another and to be praised.

The positive adjectives concept is a team-building skill we want each group to achieve, and it should be reinforced after the completion of the first team-building challenges. As the groups develop team-building skills, you may choose to eliminate this activity as a requirement.

Figure 2.1 Use positive adjectives.

Negative Pressure and Put-downs

The warm-up has let your students practice giving and receiving praise, using first names, and describing others positively. Ideally, these skills will grow as students start physical challenges.

Your students also should know about negative pressure and how it differs from a put-down. Explain that negative pressure need not be verbal; a frown or an impatient look can send the message. Both of these actions can cause pressure while a person is performing. How would you feel if someone said to you, "Come on, Paul; we all made it and we are waiting for you.''? You probably would try to accomplish the challenge, but while performing you would be more concerned about how your teammates felt about you than accomplishing the task. If you failed, you would feel terrible.

Show your students that how you say something can be as important as what you say. Have your students give examples of what they believe is negative pressure. Inform your students that positive team encouragement will help get the job done much better than negative pressure.

A put-down is a specific and deliberate attempt to make someone feel bad by saying something like "Hey, Sherry, we don't want you on our team. You can't do anything.'' That won't make Sherry happy, nor should it make the speaker feel good. Every teammate needs to feel positive about the team. Put-downs and negative pressure hurt, not help, the team.

Organizing the Challenges

Before starting a physical challenge, put the students into groups of 6 to 10 and have each group give itself a creative name. We require teams to use positive names—no names like The No Minds or Brain Tumors. We prefer something like The Einsteins, Walking Encyclopedias, or Magnificent Minds. Again, the students will have to interact, communicate, and agree—this time on a group name.

Student Responsibilities

Each team should select a member to fill these responsibilities: *organizer*, *praiser*, *encourager*, *summarizer*, and *recorder*. These assignments can rotate with every challenge.

Organizer

As each task begins, the organizer will receive two cards: an *organizer card* and a *challenge card*. These cards are integral parts of each challenge because they are the only sources of information for group members. Give a copy of each card to the organizer before a challenge begins. (These cards can be found in the appendix of this book. Please copy and laminate each card.)

The *challenge card* lists equipment to be used, the challenge, and rules and *sacrifices* of each challenge. A sacrifice is a consequence of breaking a rule. For instance, it may mean that a successful challenge solver must start over because another team member broke a rule or that the entire group must start over.

The *organizer card* includes questions the organizer will ask team members to help them understand each challenge. A team cannot start a challenge until it can answer all questions correctly. After the team answers the questions, the challenge begins. The instructor enforces the rules on the organizer card.

The team tries to solve the challenge. If the group becomes stumped, the organizer can ask the instructor for tips. Remember, though, that by giving too much help you defeat the purpose. Let the team go as far as it can before you step in to help.

Praiser

We hope everyone in the group will use Praise Phrases, but the praiser is assigned to find specific acts to praise, which are identified after the completion of the challenge.

Encourager

An encourager also acknowledges effort, and many times this role overlaps the praiser. An encourager must use positive encouragement while a teammate is attempting a challenge. The encourager's job is ongoing throughout the task. Again, we hope everyone on the team will be encouraging.

Summarizer

After each challenge, the summarizer will tell the instructor how the team solved the challenge, what was fun for the team, what was hard, and how to change the task. After all the teams have completed a specific challenge, the summarizer will tell the class how his or her team solved the challenge. The summarizer should have a team report card. (An example can be found in the appendix. Please copy and laminate.)

Recorder

The recorder highlights for the class praises and encouragement used during the challenge.

Instructor Responsibilities

The instructor needs to avoid solving the challenges. It is very tempting to help each team, but members need to learn how to function when the going gets difficult. Let them struggle. Allow them to fail before you give in to an organizer's request for help.

When setting up equipment, use all available safety precautions, including plenty of mats. Study the figures in this book and know where to place mats. Also discourage horseplay.

Be a good observer, encourager, and praiser, and do everything possible to eliminate negative team pressure.

Be ready to adapt when necessary, but enforce rules and sacrifices for the challenges. Don't be afraid to be creative. You don't have to use an organizer card to describe a challenge. Use your imagination. For instance, if you want to put a time limit on the Grand Canyon activity (Chapter 5) you could say: "Okay, Magnificent Minds, your task is to get everyone from this cliff to the other cliff before the storm hits in 15 minutes. You are stranded on this cliff and one of your members is injured. The only way your team can get to the other cliff and down the mountain is by swinging across the canyon on this vine." Don't be afraid to put alligators in the water or storms on the horizon to introduce any other hazard that will make a challenge more interesting.

Yearly Organization

As we have said, challenges fit into a curriculum in many ways. We find that beginning a school year with a few challenges sets a positive atmosphere within the class that carries into later units of study. After the fall outdoor units, we do a few more challenges. Then, after a couple of months of indoor activities, the students are eager to try more challenges. You will find that cooperation and teamwork learned in the challenges carry into the established curriculum.

Another way to present the challenges is as a unit. Try to include as many challenges as you can in a one- to two-week time span.

However you present the challenges, you will quickly find them popular with students.

Class Organization

Here are two ways to present the challenges: Set up one challenge for all groups, or set up several challenges and let the teams rotate. If you select the second method, make sure you have enough equipment.

If you set up five or six challenge stations in your gym and if your class has three or four groups, you will always have challenge stations open to receive the next group.

It should take no more than two class periods to do the warm-ups described previously in this chapter. Remember, the warm-up was designed to practice Praise Phrases, to use positive adjectives, and to function as a team. After you have done the Create-A-Game or team workout or both, you may want to structure a class period like this:

- Team placements and assignments—2 minutes
- Team workout, stretching, or other exercises (if needed)—5 to 8 minutes
- Physical challenges—15 to 20 minutes
- Positive adjectives or summarizer (if needed)—3 minutes

If a team does not finish a challenge, let it try again next class period. A team may need three class periods to solve a challenge.

Gym Setup

We have chosen six challenges to illustrate gym setup:

- Quicksand (Chapter 4)
- Stepping Stones I (Chapter 3)
- The Grand Canyon (Chapter 5)
- Alphabet Balance Beam (Chapter 3)
- River Crossing (Chapter 3)
- The Tire Bridge (Chapter 3)

These challenges range from introductory to difficult. As you can see from figure 2.2, six challenges are spaced around the gymnasium with ample room at each station. Teams rotate to an open station after completing one challenge.

These six challenges will provide activity for an average-sized class of 24-32 students, 6 to 10 group members on a team. Try to leave the equipment up for a week so all teams can rotate without having to move equipment each day. Once all groups have mastered a challenge, move to a new task.

If teams are kept together, positive adjectives are not necessary after each challenge. It's best, in fact, to keep groups together for at least a week so they can develop team-building skills with familiar teammates. If you change teammates use positive adjectives after each challenge.

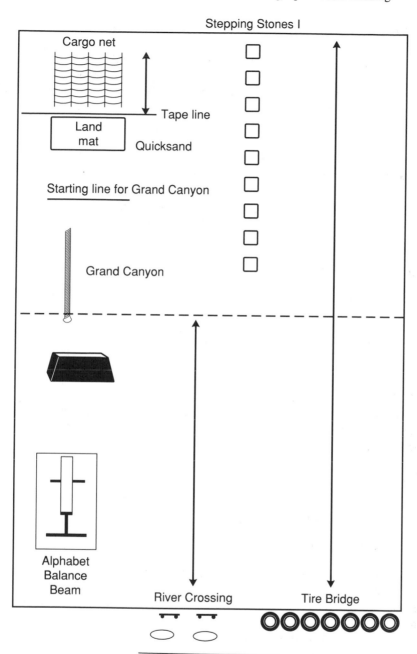

Figure 2.2 Sample station circuit.

Adaptations for Special Children and Situations

The positive concept of mainstreaming means more children with physical and mental disabilities are entering physical education classrooms. Team building is an excellent way to mainstream these students into group activities. Can you imagine how children with special needs feel when they accomplish a physical challenge? Can you imagine how a group feels when it helps a special child accomplish a challenge?

Use good judgment and understand that not all children with disabilities can accomplish every task. Involve special students as much as possible but modify each task by providing rest areas, shorter distances, and physical help from team members. Allow special students to struggle, to work with the team to solve the task, and to fail. Having a child with special needs in a group can enhance the teamwork lesson.

Resolving Conflicts

Children, like adults, have personality conflicts. Some are aggressive and domineering. Some may not bathe regularly. Counseling may be necessary, but we have found that during team building, personality conflicts diminish. You, as teambuilder, should assure that children don't badger or tease each other.

Teacher, Prepare Thyself

Use the Instructor Preparation Form in the appendix to review challenges you use. It serves as a quick reference while you are in the gymnasium or work area.

Safety First

Please review the safety notes in each challenge and add safety measures particularly necessary in your gym for your group.

Time to Get Started

You are ready to start physical challenges. We recommend you start with easier challenges and progress to advanced tasks as team building strengthens. Introductory, intermediate, and advanced challenges are detailed in the next three chapters.

We hope you will enjoy physical challenges. We know your students will love and look forward to them.

Before you begin, remember some important concepts:

1. Safety first. If you have an open area on the floor, "mat it." Don't let imagination overrule common sense. If you do not think a challenge is safe, either don't do it or make it safer.

2. Adjust heights, distances, obstacles, and difficulty to match your students' developmental levels.
3. Be positive, enthusiastic, and encouraging. Teach your students to be the same. Remind them to use Praise Phrases and positive adjectives after selected challenges.

Chapter 3

Introductory Challenges

Achieving success is like climbing a mountain. You can stand off from afar, and glimpse the summit. But if you are wise, you will quickly turn away from any such contemplation and start organizing yourself, and get on the way.

Percy Cerutty
College track coach

Alphabet Balance Beam

The most critical aspect of achieving a goal is not whether we achieved it, but rather the knowledge we gained during the process of achieving.

Glover & Midura

The alphabet balance beam, one of our favorite tasks, requires group members to help each other as they alphabetize themselves while remaining on top of a high balance beam. The students cannot touch the floor or supporting legs of the balance beam during this challenge.

Description

Group members try to rearrange themselves alphabetically. They begin by sitting in random order on the beam, as in figure 3.1. Give group members numbers to help them remember the starting order. Before the students read their instructions (the challenge card), the teacher first specifies

1. whether the students will be alphabetized right to left or left to right and
2. the name to be used for the alphabetical order, such as proper name, middle name, last name, mother's first name, father's first name, etc.

Figure 3.1 The alphabet balance beam starting position.

Success Criteria

The challenge is mastered when all group members are standing on top of the balance beam in assigned alphabetical order.

Equipment

You'll need a high balance beam, 8 to 10 tumbling mats, and one or two crash pads if they are available to you. Cover the entire working area with tumbling mats.

Setup

Choose a space away from walls or other equipment. Place two unfolded mats on the floor, end to end, and set the balance beam on the mats as shown in figure 3.2. Place one or two tumbling mats between the beam's support legs to cover any leg extensions touching the floor. Use more mats to cover the outside of the beam's legs. Place mats or crash pads behind where the group will stand on the beam. Make sure the working area is safe.

As students begin, they need to discuss which names (first, middle, last, etc.) they will use in the task. You may need to help some students spell some names. The students need to communicate how they need help and how they can help someone.

Figure 3.2 The alphabet balance beam equipment.

Rules and Sacrifices

1. All group members must remain on the beam during the task.
2. If any person touches a mat, the floor, or the legs of the beam, the entire group must get off the beam and start over.
3. If anyone calls another by last name or uses a put-down, the entire group starts over.

Possible Solutions

In solving this challenge, group members often hold tightly to the balance beam while another student steps carefully over them as shown in figure 3.3.

Figure 3.3 The alphabet balance beam challenge.

Some students will try to change positions while everyone is standing, and you may even see some maneuver under the beam. Some group members probably will lose their balance, so it is important that group members guard against a fall; no one should be deliberately careless.

If group members help one another, this task is easier; some will need additional support just to maintain their balance while sitting.

Conclusion of the Task

When the task is complete, the group is standing on the beam in the correct order as shown in figure 3.4. But standing up on the beam may be harder than alphabetizing. Students will need to plan how to stand and how to support each other. Don't be surprised to see a group make errors at this stage.

Then, when the entire group is standing, have the group recite the names used to achieve the alphabetical order. Have group members recheck their alphabetized names before they stand.

Additions and Variations

You may need to experiment to find the height at which the beam should be set so that students can not touch the mats with their feet while sitting on the balance beam. Also, when assigning order, see that the group members are not already seated alphabetically. Vary the direction of order often so that students can't anticipate. If a group has to change only a few places to achieve success, the task becomes less challenging and less fun.

Figure 3.4 The alphabet balance beam success.

River Crossing

Successful teams are proud of their accomplishments. They recognize that these accomplishments are not a matter of luck but the direct result of hard work. The responsible teammate does not blame others or make excuses when things go wrong or when the team fails to reach its goal.

Anonymous

River Crossing is a physical challenge that requires a group to cross over a designated space. In this task the group travels across a "river" (half the length of a gymnasium or basketball court) using two scooters, two deck tennis rings, and a long jump rope.

Description

All group members must get from the clearly marked beginning shore or land area across the river to the opposite shore as shown in figure 3.5. They must use the designated equipment when attempting to cross the river and cannot touch the river with any part of their bodies. All floor space between the shores is considered river.

Figure 3.5 The river crossing challenge.

Success Criteria

The task is mastered when all group members have successfully crossed the river without touching it. All designated equipment must cross the river as well.

Equipment

You'll need two sitting scooters, two deck tennis rings, and one long jump rope. (A 14- to 16-foot sash cord jump rope is recommended.) See figure 3.6. Starting and finishing lines are also necessary; they can be taped lines or the end boundary and midcourt lines of a basketball court. The space to be used should be free from obstacles or structural hazards.

Figure 3.6 The river crossing equipment.

Setup

The starting and finishing lines should be clearly marked, and the equipment should be laying at the starting line. Set one deck tennis ring on each scooter, and fold the jump rope and lay it across the two scooters. Although this challenge can be done in half a gymnasium space, a wide working area is helpful, such as half the width of a basketball court as well as half the length.

Team members travel across the river using the scooters. The rope can be used to pull someone on a scooter, and the deck tennis rings can be used to help propel the scooters or can be tied to the rope to create a better pulling device. Usually students will try to give their teammates a push start on the scooters to get them part way across the river.

Safety note: Group members must be careful not to push a teammate on a scooter so hard that he or she falls forward.

Rules and Sacrifices

1. The river is all area between the designated lines.
2. If any part of a person's body touches the river (floor), that person and another who has successfully crossed the river must be sacrificed, and those two must start over.
3. The first person across the river cannot be sacrificed. Your group will be able to keep one person across the river for the remainder of the challenge.
4. If a person touches the river while trying to rescue equipment, a sacrifice is required.
5. A sacrifice is required if last names or put-downs are used.
6. Although the first teammate successfully across the river cannot be sacrificed, that person is not allowed to touch the river. If that happens, one who later crosses successfully must be sacrificed in place of the first person.

Possible Solutions

Here is a common solution to this challenge: One person goes part way across the river on a scooter and uses one or two deck tennis rings to push the rest of the way across. The first person tries to push the scooter back across the river and rolls the deck tennis ring back to the waiting group. If the first person did not take the jump rope across, group members will throw the rope to the first teammate safely over the river. Those who successfully cross the river can then throw out the jump rope as a lifeline to pull other group members across.

Safety note: When returning equipment to the starting area, group members must take care not to hit others with it. For example, a teammate should not give an empty scooter a mighty push back across the river.

The rope is intended to be used as a transferring device, not as a tightrope. When group members attempt to walk across the rope, they cannot help but touch the floor with their shoes.

Conclusion of the Task

When the task is solved, all group members are across the river at the ending line, and all equipment designated for this task also has been brought to the ending line.

Additions and Variations

If the width of the river is greater than 35 to 40 feet, you may wish to use two long ropes or one long rope and one short rope. If the width is less than 35 feet, two long ropes make the task too easy. Make sure the combined length of ropes is less than the width of the river. To make the challenge more difficult, add obstacles in the river. These obstacles could create path diversions, or they could require sacrifices if touched. You could also require group members to carry an object such as a stuffed animal with them. Or require the group to return safely across the river to the starting line.

A group may sometimes want to use the deck tennis rings as skates. If you do not want them to use the rings in this manner, specify that in the list of rules.

The Rock

A successful team develops a positive atmosphere. Each teammate knows how to contribute. Each teammate knows that the team comes first.

Glover & Midura

The Rock challenge appears simple, but it requires the group to balance for a specified amount of time on an object (the rock). The object you use as the rock determines the difficulty of this challenge.

Description

All group members must balance on the rock (or be off the floor) for a slow count of "one-and-two-and-three-and-four-and-five." The group needs to find a way to help each other maintain balance; that could mean group members will experience close encounters with one another.

Success Criteria

The challenge is mastered when the entire group is on the rock (or off the floor) for a slow count of five. The instructor must see the task completed and is the person who counts to five.

Equipment

You'll need a rock (a 13-inch automobile tire or a heavy-duty box) and several tumbling mats to be placed under the rock. The size of the tire used in this challenge can make a significant difference in difficulty. So use smaller tires for smaller-sized groups. A large group (such as 10 group members) may need a 14- or 15-inch tire.

Setup

This task does not require much room, but you should place the tumbling mat far enough away from walls or other objects so that should a student fall, chance of injury is lessened. The mat should be unfolded (we suggest a 5- by 10-foot mat). Place the rock in the center of the mat as in figure 3.7.

Most groups first believe this task is too easy. But success does not always come quickly. Because this task requires students to hold on to one another closely (see figure 3.8), some students will debate if death is more desirable than touching someone of the opposite sex. Others will love the close encounter.

Figure 3.7 The rock equipment.

Rules and Sacrifices

1. All group members must be off the floor (tumbling mat) and on the rock.
2. All group members do not have to be touching the rock as long as they are off the floor.
3. Once you have been on the rock, touching the floor (or mat) for even an instant means the group must start over with no one on the rock.
4. No last names or put-downs may be used.

Please note the mat is to be considered part of the floor space. Once a group member gets off the floor or mat, that person should not step down onto the floor or mat, or else a sacrifice occurs.

The group needs to practice until it is confident it will succeed when it calls the instructor to witness the solution.

Possible Solutions

Most groups step onto the rock, hold on to one another tightly, start counting to five, and fall over. After a few such failures, the group learns it must plan

Figure 3.8 Meeting the rock challenge.

to step onto the rock and hold on to others while maintaining balance. One method is to hold on to someone directly across from you on the rock. As more group members get onto the rock, balancing becomes more difficult. Some groups try to have everyone put one foot on the rock and then all add the second foot on the count of three. Some group members may try to stand in the middle of the rock and have others surround them. Or a group may try to lie horizontally on the rock and on top of one another. Another group might try to sit on teammates' shoulders as they step onto the rock. Discourage this last solution because it is unsafe.

As groups practice, remind them that rule 3 is very specific. It is likely that a student will start to fall, barely touch the mat, and pop back onto the rock. If anyone touches the mat for even an instant, all group members must get off the rock and start over.

As we said, some students, especially some in upper elementary grades, may find touching one another difficult. Tell them that this task cannot be completed without physically helping one another. Reinforce positive group behavior and students will find satisfaction when a group works well together.

Conclusion of the Task

When group members have practiced their solution and are confident they can succeed, they should call the teacher to the working area. The teacher will begin the slow count of five when all group members' feet are off the floor. Even though the actual conclusion takes only five seconds, the cheering lasts longer.

Additions and Variations

To vary this challenge, you may choose to lengthen the time limit. Or you may wish to use a smaller tire (such as an 11- or 12-inch boat trailer tire). One last note: A 13-inch tire works well as a rock. A variation that adds to the difficulty of the task is to consider the hole in the tire as part of the floor. To compensate, let the students place their feet inside the tire without touching the floor. To ease the challenge for a large group or a group having considerable difficulty, count the center of the tire as part of the rock.

The Snake

Don't worry. Be happy. When you are doing the best you know how to do, you are succeeding.

Glover

The Snake is a shape-building challenge using a tug-of-war rope as the material to create the desired shapes. After the group members create a shape with the rope, they must cover the rope with their bodies. This challenge should be considered an easy one to solve, but it will take time to create the number of shapes assigned.

Description

Group members begin this challenge using either a large open space or a floor space covered by tumbling mats or carpeting. The tug-of-war rope is placed in the middle of the working space, coiled. The group either is given a list of shapes by the teacher, or the group may negotiate with the teacher to build other shapes. We suggest the groups each make eight different shapes such as numbers, letters, names, words, or designs. See figure 3.9.

Figure 3.9 The snake shape challenge.

Success Criteria

The challenge is mastered when the group completes the number of shapes the teacher has assigned. All group members must be part of each shape created. The tug-of-war rope must be completely covered by the group members each time a shape is created. Each shape will be considered completed when approved by the teacher.

Equipment

One tug-of-war rope is needed.

Setup

All you need is a large open space although you may wish to cover the floor with tumbling mats. Place the tug-of-war rope in the center of the working space as in figure 3.10. Curl the rope into a coil.

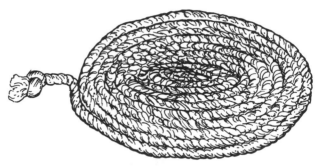

Figure 3.10 A tug-of-war rope.

Rules and Sacrifices

1. Make the shape using a tug-of-war rope.
2. All group members must lie on the rope.
3. The tug-of-war rope must be completely covered by group members.
4. The group must have each shape approved by the teacher before beginning another shape.
5. No last names or put-downs.

There are no sacrifices for this challenge, but you should require the group members to form clearly identifiable shapes to gain approval.

Possible Solutions

Group members find certain shapes, letters, or numbers very easy to build. You may wish to include some easy, moderate, and difficult shapes in their assignment. Groups may find the rope longer than the combined lengths of their bodies. It may take them some time to discern that they can double the rope over if necessary.

Conclusion of the Task

The challenge is solved when group members form the designated number of assigned shapes such as the one in figure 3.11. The group should leave the rope in a neat coil at the center of the working area for the next group.

Figure 3.11 The snake letter "S."

Additions and Variations

If you do not have a tug-of-war rope, jump ropes tied together or clothesline rope 40 to 50 feet long could be substituted. Electrical cords 50 to 100 feet long could also be used. (Please don't plug them in!)

If you use simple or familiar shapes, you may wish to add time limits to each task and award points for reaching certain goals. Or you could have groups compete in a timed activity. You could combine groups and create extra-large projects. Displaying pictures of a successful group making its shapes would motivate that group and others.

This challenge presents virtually no safety problems, but remind the group not to step on one another when finding their place.

Stepping Stones I

Individual commitment to a group effort, that is what makes a team work, a company work, a society work, a civilization work.

Vince Lombardi

Stepping Stones I can be a difficult challenge to master but it offers groups many solutions. This task's difficulty lies in the reluctance of most students to touch someone physically. Verbal communication is exceptionally important in solving this challenge. We have in fact included it as an introductory challenge because of its value in teaching group decision making.

In this task, students stand in specific order, using bases set in a straight line, then reverse their order by moving from base to base.

Description

Lay out on the floor a straight line of bases, 12 to 15 inches apart as in figure 3.12. The students begin on a base, then move from base to base until they are in reverse order from their starting positions. Use one more base than you have group members (*e.g.*, if eight students, use nine bases) so students can shift positions. Group members need to help one another move and maintain their balance, which is vital to this task.

Figure 3.12 The stepping stones I challenge.

Success Criteria

The challenge is mastered when the group is standing in reverse order from its starting position. See figure 3.13.

Figure 3.13 Mastering the stepping stones I challenge.

For example:

Starting position:
Sally — Luke — Tasha — Megan — Matt — Ericka — Ann — Seth
Ending position:
Seth — Ann — Ericka — Matt — Megan — Tasha — Luke — Sally

Equipment

You'll need one base for each group member plus one extra base. See figure 3.14. (Have extra bases available to handle large groups.) Flat, indoor bases are best. If you have no bases, tape 12- to 15-inch squares on the floor or use carpet squares cut to that size.

Figure 3.14 Stepping stones I equipment.

Setup

Outline the bases with tape so the students know where the bases belong and so the bases are more likely to remain stationary. This also helps you set up the task for the next class or the next day.

It may be helpful for students to take a number (1, 2, 3, 4, 5, 6, 7, 8) to help them remember their positions at the end of the challenge.

Rules and Sacrifices

This task has more rules than any other task in this book. So the group needs extra time for reading.

1. Only one person may touch a base at one time.
2. When moving from base to base, a person may move in either direction to a neighboring base.
3. Group members may touch a new base only if it is empty.
4. The bases may not be moved except for minor adjustments; no penalty is necessary if the group member does not get off the base to adjust it.
5. Shoes are considered part of the person. (That means shoes may not be removed, be put on the floor, or be used as extra stepping stones.)
6. No one may touch the floor with any part of the body.
7. If any rule is broken, the entire group must start the task again.

The rule against more than one group member touching the same base at the same time does not mean a group member cannot lift or hold another off an occupied base or step on the feet of teammates to move along.

Possible Solutions

In the most common solution to this challenge, a person on one end works toward the other end by jumping or stepping over neighbors, who squat as low as possible. The student on the move of course, needs an empty base upon which to step. Look back at the example under Success Criteria for this challenge. The group needs to leave an empty base between Ann and Ericka so that Seth has a base to move to. Ann gets as low as possible so that Seth can step or leap over her. Ericka prepares to help Seth keep his balance. (Another approach: Ann and Seth could exchange positions.) After Seth goes by, Ann moves to the end base where Seth began. Seth moves over next to Ann, and Ericka moves next to Seth, leaving an empty base between Ericka and Matt. Seth tries to get past Ericka to the next position and Matt prepares to assist Seth. The group continues this procedure until Seth makes it to the opposite end of the line. Then it's Ann's turn. She moves down the line until she is next to Seth. Then it's Ericka's turn, then Matt's, then Megan's, etc., until the group has fully reversed its order.

Rather than jump or step over each other, teammates could step on their neighbor's shoes (without touching the base) and move to the next base. Group members could lift one another over to a new base. Leap-frogging over one another is another option.

Regardless of the method used, teammates need to help each other maintain their balance so that no one touches the floor or touches a base already occupied. The size of the bases allows little margin of error for maintaining one's balance. Groups working well together will have nonmoving members reaching toward their teammates to physically support them.

A difficulty observed in this challenge is that when a group member makes an error, the group abandons its first plan and attempts a different solution. Another problem can arise when a group attempts an improbable method (such as crawling over the backs of teammates squatting down) but does not quickly see the futility of its efforts.

Conclusion of the Task

When the task is solved, group members will be standing on the bases in reverse order of their starting positions (cheering joyfully, of course).

Additions and Variations

Variations have been covered in the section on possible solutions. Groups that do not work well together find this is a difficult challenge, but groups willing to help each other can do this task quickly. It is fun to see teammates helping each other!

Teamwork Walk

You can't do it alone. Be a team player, not an individualist, and respect your teammates. Anything you do, you'll have to do as a team. Many records have been made, but only because of the help of one's teammates.

Charley Taylor
Former NFL wide receiver
From "The Edge" by Howard Ferguson

The Teamwork Walk challenge is easy to figure out but hard to do. It is fun for groups to solve, but it requires practice and teamwork. Every group member plays an equal role in solving the task.

Description

The group tries to follow a designated path, usually the length or perimeter of a basketball court. The group uses team skis, made of long two-by-six boards with footholds so that group members can secure their feet. You will need to construct the team skis because they are not commercially made. (See Equipment.)

Success Criteria

The challenge is mastered when the group has completed the designated path without touching the floor or wall with any part of their bodies. The path can vary in length or difficulty depending on the space you have available and the ages of group members.

Equipment

The group uses team skis or long walking boards such as those shown in figure 3.15. The equipment is not available in physical education supply or equipment catalogs; you will need to have it made. You will need two 12-foot two-by-six pine or fir boards. (Length can vary to meet your needs.) You also need No. 12 sash cord, clothesline rope, or strapping material to make the footholds.

Drill holes through the two-by-sixes so that the rope or strapping material can pass through the boards. If the holes are drilled about 18 inches apart,

Figure 3.15 The teamwork walk equipment.

you will be able to fit eight sets of footholds on a 12-foot board. By using heavier rope or by crisscrossing the rope, you can make the footholds more secure and give the group members better support. Group members should be able to easily remove their feet from the skis when they fall.

Setup

Just provide the group a set of team skis and a designated walking path. The path should be long enough to make the challenge interesting. Remember that the skis will be somewhere from 8 to 12 feet long, so choose a space that allows for a long enough challenge and adequate turning space.

Rules and Sacrifices

1. Group members may not touch the floor with any part of the body.
2. Group members may not use walls or stationary structures to help them maintain their balance.
3. If a rule is broken, the group starts over.
4. No last names or put-downs can be used.

Possible Solutions

Teamwork is the solution for this challenge. Using a group leader or organizer helps because someone must coordinate the team's movements. For instance, team members must move their feet simultaneously. It helps to have someone count cadence. Group members should physically assist one another, by holding on to the hips, waist, or shoulders of the group member directly in front. See figure 3.16. On turns, clear verbal communication is essential. Be aware that if one person falls during the task, others may too. Deliberate carelessness could result in teammates being put into precarious positions.

Figure 3.16 The teamwork walk challenge.

Conclusion of the Task

The group is successful when it crosses the finish line. (It is your decision whether a team finishes when the first person reaches the end or when the entire team crosses the end.)

Additions and Variations

This challenge is open to a variety of additions or variations. As you observe your groups perform this challenge, we are sure you will find variations we have not tried.

- The challenge must be completed within a time limit.
- Use both a time limit and distance goal. How far can the group travel in a given time? A large gymnasium or long hall lends itself well to this variation.
- Devise an obstacle course or zig-zag path, or require specific turns as variations. A 360-degree turn might be a very tough challenge.
- Don't let students hold on to one another. This variation should not be attempted with younger students.
- Set a number of objects along the path to be picked up, such as a ball, jump rope, base, or hoop. The team stops to let the teammates pick up one object each.
- Send the group members under a lowered parallel bar or a volleyball net while walking.

This challenge generates a lot of laughter and fun.

The Whole World in Their Hands

The only way for a team to succeed is to work at it. Intensity is essential to team success. Your team will never reach its goal by wishing for it to happen. Set your team goal and direct your efforts totally to attaining it.
Dr. Dennis Waitley, "The Psychology of Winning"

This challenge, one of the newer tasks we use, offers several solutions. This challenge can be solved quickly if a group works well together (and has some good luck); it also can be a challenge hard to master. This task also requires the group to move or use body parts in ways quite different from other challenges. This is a good introductory challenge.

Description

The group tries to transfer a large cage ball (48 inches in diameter or larger) from one end of a gymnasium to the other, a distance of 45 to 60 feet. The larger the ball, the more interesting the challenge. The cage ball starts out resting on an automobile tire. The goal is to move the ball to a second tire at the other end of the gym. The group has to move the ball without letting it touch the floor and without touching it with their hands or arms.

Success Criteria

The challenge is mastered when the students move the cage ball from tire 1, transfer it across the gymnasium space, and balance it on the second tire. You may wish to add the condition that the group members hoist the cage ball above their heads. (Of course, they would be allowed to use their hands for this activity once the ball has been balanced on tire 2.) The cage ball may not touch the floor.

Equipment

You'll need two automobile tires, one large cage ball (48 inches in diameter or larger), and a long, open gymnasium space. See figure 3.17. A large earth ball (commercially sold) could be substituted for the cage ball. The ball should be inflated to the maximum size possible.

Figure 3.17 The whole world equipment.

Setup

Choose an open working space because it is likely some groups will use the crab walk position and could bump into walls. The large ball also will be easier to control away from walls.

Group members start by sitting around the cage ball in a crab walk position. They may sit on the floor. During the challenge, they may move to other positions.

Rules and Sacrifices

1. The cage ball cannot touch the floor.
2. The cage ball cannot touch the hands or arms of any group member.
3. If a rule is broken, the ball must be returned to tire 1 and the group must begin the task again.
4. No last names or put-downs can be used.

Possible Solutions

We've found multiple solutions to this challenge, and undoubtedly you and your students will find others. We offer four solutions.

1. Group members lift the cage ball off tire 1 with their feet and crab walk or slide across the gymnasium floor; they use feet, legs, and upper bodies to keep the ball from rolling over the group members and onto the floor. When the team gets the cage ball to the second tire, it lifts the ball onto the tire, again using all body parts except hands and arms as shown in figure 3.18.

Figure 3.18 The whole world walking together.

2. Group members lay in two lines similar to railroad tracks. See figure 3.19. Two group members roll the ball down the lines of bodies, using their bodies to keep the ball from rolling onto the floor. As the cage ball moves, the people on the floor adjust their positions to lengthen the lines. When the cage ball gets near tire 2, at least four group members should be in position to help get the ball onto the tire.

3. Similarly, group members lay on the floor, side by side, but this time like railroad ties. See figure 3.20. Again, at least two group members guide

Figure 3.19 The whole world railroad tracks.

Figure 3.20 The whole world railroad ties.

the ball across the bodies of the group members, and the group members adjust their positions after the ball crosses them to extend the line.

4. The team stands with backs to the ball while one or two group members try to raise the ball high enough with their legs so that their teammates can press against the ball with their backs. The group then tries to walk the ball to tire 2. The teammates who raised the ball with their legs quickly join the group to help control the ball.

Conclusion of the Task

Success is achieved when the group rests the cage ball on tire 2. You may wish to end the challenge by having group members lift the ball above their heads. Figure 3.21 shows the option of singing "We've Got the Whole World in Our Hands."

Figure 3.21   The whole world success.

Additions and Variations

Consider allowing younger students limited use of hands or arms.

To encourage students to think for themselves, you may want to require a group to find a solution different from another group's solution.

Asking students to move the ball from the end back to the starting tire, either using the first solution or a different method, is a good task that requires participation by everyone in the group.

The Tire Bridge

The challenges of the next few decades are going to be people and process-oriented. Knowing how to communicate with and relate to others is going to be a fundamental skill.

Shelly Freeman
Educational consultant

The Tire Bridge is another challenge in which a group moves from one end of a large space such as a gymnasium to the other. The group uses automobile tires to construct a moving bridge. This task is time consuming but not difficult.

Description

The group uses tires to create a moving bridge to cross a river.

Success Criteria

The task is mastered when all group members have crossed the river and stand together with the tires stacked vertically.

Equipment

You'll need one tire per group member plus one additional tire such as those shown in figure 3.22. Large tires are harder to move and therefore create more physical work for a group. Small tires, such as boat trailer tires, are easier to move, but may be harder on which to balance. Clean the tires before use. Bias-ply tires, hard to find these days, are less likely to have problems such as exposed belts or threads. Beginning and ending lines will also be necessary (usually the boundary lines of a basketball court).

Figure 3.22 The tire bridge equipment.

Setup

Place the tires near the starting position. If a basketball court or similar space is used, provide a clear path. The ending position should have enough space so students can stand "on land" and stack the tires in a column also on land. This challenge does not present safety concerns if the group stays away from equipment and walls.

Because this task is not too difficult physically, group members need to encourage one another to concentrate. Broken concentration can mean breaking rules 3 and 4, which follow.

Rules and Sacrifices

1. The students must begin standing on land.
2. Only one person may be on one tire at a time.
3. If any group member touches the river (the floor) with any part of the body, the bridge must be moved back to the starting position.
4. If two people step on one tire at the same time, the bridge must be moved back to the start.
5. If last names or put-downs are used, the group starts over.

Possible Solutions

As they step on the tires and form a line with the tires, group members pass the last tire to the front of the line, and, one by one, group members step forward. See figure 3.23. Some groups carefully lay the tires on the floor ahead; daring groups may toss the tires forward. If group members do not coordinate their moves, someone may step on an occupied tire, causing the group to start over.

Figure 3.23 The tire bridge challenge.

A group may lose control of a tire. A student can place both feet inside the tire and jump toward the runaway tire, but it would be difficult and tiring for the entire group to travel across the river this way.

Conclusion of the Task

Success is achieved when group members have crossed the river and have stacked the tires vertically as in figure 3.24. Group members cannot step into the river. After you approve the group's accomplishment, have members carry the tires back to the starting position.

Figure 3.24 The tire bridge success.

Additions and Variations

Here are some ways to vary this task:

- The group could be given more tires than previously to pass. This requires more physical labor.
- A time limit (such as 20 minutes) could be placed on completing the task.
- Create a zig-zag path rather than a straight line.
- Islands could be provided for resting or regrouping.

The Wall I

The basic fuel for the teamwork machine is enthusiasm.

Glover & Midura

Maybe it is just the nature of children to love climbing, but every time The Wall I challenge is used, it creates a lot of fun and excitement. This challenge requires a group to climb over a wall of mats or crash pads. It also requires the group to work together and to develop positive team-building skills.

Description

The height of the wall is important; it should be high enough to make the task challenging yet reasonable enough to keep the task safe. Getting tall or heavy group members over the wall challenges the whole group, and getting the last person over the wall is usually the most difficult aspect. If you create a wall high enough, group members must help one another.

Success Criteria

The task is mastered when the entire group has crossed the wall.

Equipment

You'll need a large folding crash pad standing on end (at least 5 by 10 feet and 12 inches thick when unfolded) and two tumbling mats (unfolded) to lay under the wall. If no crash pad is available, use a 5- to 6-foot stack of folded tumbling mats. To keep the wall from falling over, tie jump ropes or strapping material around the mats or crash pads.

Setup

A 15- by 15-foot space away from walls and equipment is enough for this challenge. First, lay two unfolded mats on the floor side by side (not end to end). Stand the crash pad on end with the sides folded inward. Center the crash pad on the two mats. Tie jump ropes or strapping material around the crash pad so that it does not come apart. Mark a dividing line on the floor, dividing the wall. See figure 3.25. The students cannot cross the line unless they go over the wall.

Rules and Sacrifices

1. The crash pad may not fall over.
2. Students may not grasp crash pad handles or ropes holding the crash pad together.
3. Students may not step over the line dividing the mats into two sections.
4. If rule 1 is broken, the entire group must start over.
5. If either rule 2 or rule 3 is broken, the person making the error and one person already across the wall must start over.
6. If last names or put-downs are used, the entire group must start over.

Figure 3.25 The wall I equipment.

You may see people trying to boost others over the wall or see group members on their hands and knees allowing others to step on their backs. See figure 3.26. Some group members may try to jump up on the wall, which could knock the wall over. Monitor this type of attempt and consider eliminating it if it appears unsafe or unmanageable.

Figure 3.26 The wall I challenge.

Possible Solutions

Group members need to help get each other over the wall. Because getting the last person over the wall can present the most difficulty, the group may need to keep at least one person on top of the wall to help lift the last person as in figure 3.27. If top-heavy with group members, the wall could fall over. Group members on the floor can support the wall and hold up those on top of the wall. This is enjoyable, especially for elementary students. Make safety a top priority. You could eliminate jumping down from the wall. Group members should not pull on teammates' clothing when assisting them. Besides damaging clothing, some embarrassing moments could take place.

Figure 3.27 Solving the wall I challenge.

Conclusion of the Task

The challenge is met when all group members have crossed the wall.

Additions and Variations

- To make the task more difficult, require group members to remain on the mats when they are not touching the wall. This restricts movement and prevents group members from running and jumping up to the wall.
- To promote planning, prevent group members from climbing on top of the wall to help others more than once. This would make the group plan how to help others up to the wall, how to help others climb over, and how to support those on top of the wall.

This challenge presents few safety problems, although you should make sure the wall does not fall over because of careless or reckless behavior. Students should not jump off the wall or slide off the wall head first.

Chapter 4

Intermediate Challenges

Reward teammates; give praise, recognition, a special privilege or increased responsibility for a job well done. Emphasize the good things they do, not the bad.

National PTA Magazine, 1987

Bridge Over the Raging River

Failure is only the opportunity to begin again more intelligently.

Henry Ford, American automobile manufacturer
From "The Edge" by Howard Ferguson

Bridge Over the Raging River is a terrific challenge that requires all group members to be integral parts of the solution as they cross a river using four automobile tires, two 8-foot-long boards, and two ropes. This challenge is not difficult intellectually, but most groups will find it one of the more physically difficult.

Description

All group members travel from one end of a space (land) to the other end without touching the floor (river). The length of a basketball court works well. The group must carry all the equipment to the other side.

Success Criteria

The task is mastered when all group members have successfully crossed the river without breaking the rules and with their equipment.

Equipment

You'll need four automobile tires (large tires are harder to use), two 8-foot two-by-fours, and two jump ropes (8- to 14-foot lengths of sash cord work best). See figure 4.1.

Figure 4.1 Bridge over raging river equipment.

Setup

Label distinct starting and ending lines and use a straight-line open area (the length of a gymnasium) free from any objects or walls.

The group creates a series of movable bridges using the two-by-fours to close the gaps between tires. One tire will often be used as an island for students to stand on as they transfer equipment forward. The jump ropes are tied to a tire or two-by-four to pull the equipment forward.

Safety note: Remind groups that the two-by-fours must be moved safely. This includes being careful not to accidentally hit teammates with the boards or to step on one end of a two-by-four so that it flips up.

Rules and Sacrifices

1. Group members may not touch the river (floor).
2. A group member may not step on a two-by-four if it has one end in the river (the two-by-four may sag into [touch] the river without a penalty).
3. If a rule is broken, the group must take the bridge back to the starting position and start over.
4. No last names or put-downs can be used.

Possible Solutions

Among the possible solutions for this task, most groups follow one basic pattern. The group members will make a movable bridge. See figure 4.2. As the group advances, it passes the tires and two-by-fours forward. Group members must share space on a tire.

Figure 4.2 Making a movable bridge.

Participants need good balance and need to hold on to or physically assist teammates throughout the challenge. They simply have no choice but to constantly help one another! The group also needs to communicate how it intends to pass the equipment along. If someone tries to roll a tire without the intended recipient's knowledge, the tire might roll off course, causing an unwanted detour. Some groups may attempt to move some tires by getting their feet inside the tires and jumping along with the tire (hard to do, but possible). Most groups attempting the challenge will find it difficult to have several teammates balance on a tire at once. It is very common to see multiple mistakes, which generally result in having to start the task over.

Conclusion of the Task

The successful teammates will have crossed the river (the length of the gymnasium or basketball court) with all assigned equipment in their possession as shown in figure 4.3. The instructor may institute a time limit, basing success on criteria other than crossing the river. When group members have concluded their challenge, have them bring the equipment back to the starting position for the next group to use.

Figure 4.3 Bridge over raging river success.

Additions and Variations

Smaller tires (such as boat trailer tires of 11 to 12 inches) create a very crowded area and make it more difficult for a number of people to maintain good balance. You might place obstacles (cones, balance beams, parallel bars) in the river that the group must travel around, over, or under. Another variation is to have the group carry some object (such as a football blocking dummy) pretending it is an injured group member being rescued.

The Human Billboard

Concentrate on finding your goal, then concentrate on reaching it!
Michael Friedsam, American businessman, military colonel
From "The Edge" by Howard Ferguson

In this physical challenge, students hang from a cargo net to form letters. When constructing each letter, every group member must be on the cargo net.

Description

The group will be given a list of letters—generally capitals—from which to choose. After a letter is approved, group members must get off the cargo net before the next letter is constructed. By planning on paper, the group can assign each member a specific part of the letter being constructed.

Success Criteria

Using all members in the group, the team constructs 8 of the 12 letters assigned by the teacher. The challenge is mastered when the eighth letter is completed. All letters must be constructed on the cargo net.

Equipment

You'll need a hanging cargo net, tumbling mats or crash pads for use under the cargo net for safety (two to four mats), a list of letters from which to choose, and paper and pencils for drawing plans. See figure 4.4.

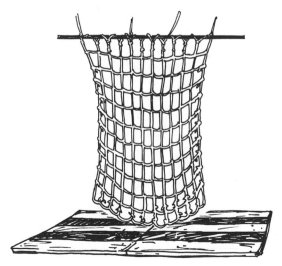

Figure 4.4 The human billboard equipment.

Setup

Lay out enough tumbling mats under the cargo net so the entire area under the net is safe. How many mats you use depends upon the size of your cargo net and the size of the floor space beneath. Provide a list of letters and paper and pencils with which group members can plan before they climb the cargo net.

Group members often choose easier letters to construct first. This encourages them. Some members may always want to climb to the top part of the cargo net, but this may not suit all teammates. As the challenge continues, be careful that no student gets too tired and becomes a safety concern. Any group member afraid of heights should remain close to the bottom of the cargo net. After approving the construction of each letter, the teacher should check that letter off the list before the next letter is constructed.

Rules and Sacrifices

1. All group members must be off the floor and on the cargo net.
2. All group members must be on the same side of the cargo net.
3. All group members must climb down from the cargo net before a new letter can be constructed.
4. All group members must use their teammates' first names only.

Possible Solutions

To solve this challenge, group members usually position themselves on the net so that their bodies become parts of the letter being built. See figure 4.5.

Figure 4.5 The human billboard challenge.

Group members assume diagonal, horizontal, or vertical positions. As an example, if seven people are constructing the letter H, three students might create a vertical line on each side, while one student makes a horizontal line across the middle. Letters with straight lines (such as E, F, H, L, and T) are easier to construct. It may benefit the group to have one member remain on the floor until the letter is just about completed. This person can correct placement of teammates on the net and suggest changes in body shapes to better form letters.

Conclusion of the Task

The group spells success when it has constructed 8 of 12 letters from the teacher's list. Group members should sit on the mats under the cargo net ready to exchange compliments.

Additions and Variations

Additions and variations to this challenge may depend on available equipment and space. If your net does not accommodate a group of seven or eight students, you might allow group members to climb on both sides of the net. If you do not have a cargo net, you could perform a variation of this task on the floor using tumbling mats. If your school has walls covered with stall bars, you could substitute the bars for the net. If your cargo net is small or if stall bars are low, you could let a group make two of the same letters rather than one large letter. You could modify rule 1 by allowing group members who form the bottom part of the letter to touch the floor.

You also may decide to make your own list, use lower-case letters, include numbers, or require fewer than eight letters for mastering the task. Another variation would be to allow the group to draw a design and then try to construct it on the net. As in all cases, modify the challenge so that it conforms to your needs, your facilities, and your equipment.

We have used a variation to Human Billboard that we call Skywriters. This task is similar but calls for shapes to be made rather than letters. You can make your own list of shapes, use shapes from a source such as an art lesson, or have students create their own shapes. Some groups will find extra motivation in creating their own shapes.

Because of the nature of this challenge, group members run the risk of stepping on teammates' hands while climbing on the net. Constant communication between group members can make them more careful when they change positions.

Generally, this challenge looks easier on paper than when tried on a cargo net. Do require that straight lines look straight and that letters with curves bend properly.

Jumping Machine

Keep away from people who try to belittle your ambitions. Small people always do that, but the really great make you feel that you, too, can become great.

Mark Twain

Jumping Machine challenges a group to complete 10 consecutive jumps over a turning tug-of-war rope.

Description

The group selects two members to turn the tug-of-war rope as they would a jump rope. Other group members try to jump the rope 10 consecutive times. The entire group (minus the turners) must jump the rope at the same time. The rope turners may change places with a jumper if a jumper needs to rest.

Success Criteria

The group masters the challenge when all members complete 10 consecutive jumps without a miss or without stopping the rope between jumps.

Equipment

You'll need one long tug-of-war rope (see figure 4.6) and a space large enough to safely turn the rope as a jump rope. Because a tug-of-war rope is long, you may need the space of up to half a basketball court. If you do not have a tug-of-war rope, tie two long jump ropes together. (Ropes made of sash cord are recommended rather than speed ropes.) If you have enough rope, you might try tying ropes parallel to one another, making a strand two or three ropes thick and about 25 to 30 feet long.

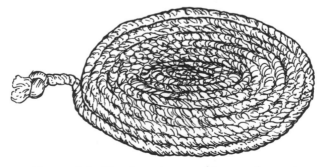

Figure 4.6 The jumping machine equipment.

Setup

Many groups assume this is an easy challenge, and for some it may be. But to be successful, the group needs a plan for entering the turning rope and may also need to have a number of group members practice turning the heavy rope. The jumpers can't jump well if the rope turners don't turn the rope well. Because of the weight and length of the rope, the rope will need a high arc. To accomplish this, the rope turners will need to use their upper body strength. The rope turners need not hold the tug-of-war rope at the ends, so they need to experiment turning the rope to find the best hand placement. The weight of the rope, rather than the length, is what adds difficulty to this challenge.

Rules and Sacrifices

1. There may be only one group member at each end of the rope. All other group members are jumpers.
2. To be counted, the jumps must be consecutive.
3. The rope must pass over the jumpers' heads and below their feet.
4. If they miss, jumpers begin the task again.
5. Turners do not have to hold the very end of the tug-of-war rope.
6. The team members may call teammates by first names only.

Possible Solutions

We generally find there are two solutions to this challenge. One solution has the jumpers standing in a straight line, close together (one or two feet apart). On a signal, all jumpers start jumping at the same time. See figure 4.7. The second solution has jumpers start jumping rope one or two at a time. In the second solution, the group does not start counting jumps until all team members have entered the turning rope.

Figure 4.7 The jumping machine challenge.

If the rope turners get tired or have trouble doing their job, teammates could take their place. If new turners take over, they also should have a chance to practice.

Rarely will a group be immediately successful with this challenge. It is common to find groups that, because of repeated failures, try to circumvent the rules, often by slowing the speed of the turning rope so that group members can step over the rope—slow-motion, instant-replay style. The rope needs to be turned at a challenging pace.

Conclusion of the Task

The challenge is mastered when the group completes 10 consecutive jumps. The group should count its successful jumps aloud so members always know their status. This also means the teacher won't have to watch the group all the time, because the nature of the counting usually causes students to be dependable and honest.

Additions and Variations

If you decide to tie two long jump ropes together to create one extra long one, we suggest requiring the rope turners to hold the very ends of the rope to make the challenge harder. If you have access to sash cord (this can be purchased at most hardware stores), you could cut it to 25 to 35 feet to serve as your turning rope. (Sash cord is usually sold in 100-foot hanks.)

If the group has fewer than seven people working together, this task becomes too easy. We recommend that two groups be combined for this task rather than trying it with too few participants.

Be aware that the weight of the rope hitting a jumper's feet can cause a fall. If you feel more comfortable, have your students jump on tumbling mats. Turning the rope carefully also lessens the possibility of the rope hitting someone's head.

Quicksand

Teamwork is the ability to have different thoughts about things; it's the ability to argue and say what you believe. But in the end, it's also the ability to adjust and do what is best for the team.

Tom Landry
From "The Edge" by Howard Ferguson

Quicksand can be one of the more difficult challenges. It requires a group to travel from a beginning line (land) over a wide floor space (quicksand) to another designated line (land) while swinging on a hanging cargo net. Most groups look at this challenge as both easy and fun, but they soon discover that without a good plan they might wind up taking turns failing.

Description

By using the cargo net to swing over the quicksand, the group members transport themselves across the space bounded by the starting and ending lines. The group usually uses a long jump rope to pull the cargo net toward land once it gets the first person over the quicksand. The first person will have to jump from the net to a tumbling mat on land. Because of this, the distances between starting and ending lines is important. If group members try to jump too far, they might get their feet caught in the net.

Remaining group members can be pulled over the quicksand through creative teamwork.

Success Criteria

The challenge is mastered when all group members have crossed the quicksand and are standing on a mat on the land side. Group members must use the cargo net to cross the quicksand.

Equipment

You'll need a suspended cargo net (see figure 4.8), one long jump rope, and at least four tumbling mats.

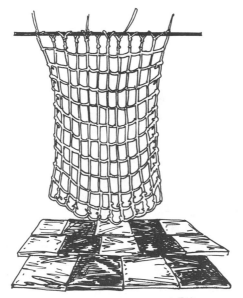

Figure 4.8 Quicksand equipment.

Setup

The cargo net needs to be hanging and can be touching the floor. Modifications for this factor can be easily made. Lay a long jump rope near the starting area. (A sash cord rope is recommended.) Mark a starting line 4 to 6 feet away from the net as it hangs motionless. If you mark the starting line with tape, make the line at least 20 feet long.

Place tape for the ending line 8 to 10 feet from the net on the side opposite the starting line. This line should lay parallel to and be the same length as the starting line. Place at least one unfolded tumbling mat behind and up to the edge of the ending line. Place enough unfolded tumbling mats under the cargo net to assure safe landings.

The distance between starting and ending lines depends on the size of the cargo net and your preference. These suggestions are offered as examples. Please experiment with this challenge before you assign it to your groups.

If the cargo net hangs near a wall, you may need to place a tumbling mat against the wall to protect group members swinging on the cargo net.

Rules and Sacrifices

1. The quicksand is the area between the starting and ending lines.
2. If a group member touches the quicksand (the floor or tumbling mats), that person and one person who has crossed the quicksand must start over.
3. If a group member who has crossed the quicksand and is standing on the land mat steps back across the ending line and into quicksand, that person and another who has crossed must start over.
4. No put-downs or last names may be used.

Possible Solutions

Groups generally start by getting control of the cargo net. To do this, someone usually jumps over the starting line and onto the net as in figure 4.9. This person swings the net so group members standing on land can reach and pull the net toward them. Once they have control of the net, they can tie the jump rope to it, although not all groups immediately use the rope. The jump rope will be used to help swing and pull the cargo net.

Getting the first person over the quicksand is the most difficult aspect of the task, and here the placement of the jump rope can become an important factor. A rope tied low (rather than high) works better. A rope tied near one side of the net works better than one tied in the middle. Group members working from an edge of the cargo net can be more successful than working from the middle of the net. The first person who successfully crosses the quicksand grabs the rope attached to the cargo net to pull it toward the ending line. Other group members jump onto the cargo net, are pulled over the quicksand, and step or jump onto the land mat. See figure 4.10.

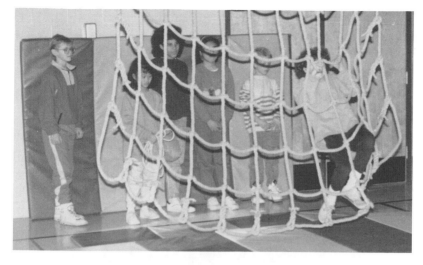

Figure 4.9 Jumping onto the net.

Figure 4.10 Pulling team members across the quicksand.

Group members getting off the cargo net need to make sure not to step into quicksand, because if they do, a sacrifice is necessary. Group members safely across the quicksand need to constantly adjust the mat on land to keep it out of the quicksand. A group member standing on a land mat that slides over the ending line is considered in quicksand.

As more group members cross the quicksand, it is much easier to pull remaining group members over. Group members also can help their teammates down from the cargo net. This challenge is difficult to get started, but once the group gets a few teammates over the quicksand, the success rate increases rapidly.

Hint: When a sacrifice is necessary, the group member returning to the starting line should be one who got over the quicksand easily.

Conclusion of the Task

When all have crossed the quicksand, the group is standing on the land mat (just beyond the end line), cheering, as in figure 4.11, you can be sure. After they have praised one another and after you approve the group's success, have them untie the rope and return it to the starting area before going on to another challenge.

Figure 4.11 Quicksand success.

Additions and Variations

Keep in mind that you need to experiment to determine the best distances to use between the lines and cargo net. The net should reach just over the ending line when pulled tight in that direction. This allows students to crawl off the cargo net without jumping (except for the first group member).

If your cargo net touches the floor so that it is difficult to swing, use another jump rope to lift and tie the cargo net off the floor.

The only effective variation to this challenge we have used is to adjust the distances between starting and ending lines. This task is very challenging, so be sure group members participate safely.

Tarzan of the Jungle

A winning team has a concentration and focus. A successful team learns from its mistakes.

Glover & Midura

Tarzan of the Jungle is a challenge that immediately gets students excited. The thought of swinging on ropes can be equaled only by getting an unexpected day off from school. Students will attempt to swing from one "cliff" (tumbling mat or vaulting box) to another "cliff" by using vines (climbing ropes). The group needs to accomplish this feat without touching the floor.

Description

The group begins by standing on cliff 1. This cliff will be either a vaulting box or a stack of tumbling mats. If tumbling mats (folded) are used, they should be stacked four or five high. At least three climbing ropes are used as the swinging vines. Group members try to swing across the "swamp," "canyon," "ravine," and so forth, to cliff 2, which is similar to cliff 1. As group members swing from rope to rope, they try to reach cliff 2 without touching the floor. When they arrive at cliff 2, they will either stay on the cliff or step onto one of two tires and assist their teammates. The distance group members swing depends on the placement of climbing ropes and the distance you set the cliffs from the vines.

Success Criteria

The challenge is mastered when all group members have swung by ropes from cliff 1 to cliff 2 without touching the floor.

Equipment

You'll need three or more climbing ropes, tumbling mats on the floor for safety, a vaulting box or stack of four to five tumbling mats for each of the two cliffs, and two automobile tires. See figure 4.12.

Setup

Begin by laying a row of unfolded tumbling mats end to end to cover the floor area the group will stand on or swing over. Build cliff 1 from a vaulting box or vertical stack of tumbling mats near rope 1. Build cliff 2 the same as cliff 1 beyond the last rope. The distance between cliffs and ropes is determined partly by existing placement of climbing ropes, by how close to a wall the ropes hang, and by the distance you believe your students can safely swing.

Figure 4.12 Tarzan of the jungle equipment.

Set two automobile tires near cliff 2. These tires can be moved by the group as long as the students do not touch the floor. The task should move away from the closest wall, toward the most open space.

Rules and Sacrifices

1. If a group member touches the floor between the cliffs, that person and one who has swung to cliff 2 must go back to the starting position.
2. If a group member falls off a cliff during the task, that person plus one successful person must go back to the starting position.
3. Teammates may stand on the tires to help support cliff 2 or other group members.
4. Do not use last names or put-downs; a person who does and one successful swinger must go back to cliff 1.

Possible Solutions

As this challenge begins, all group members stand on cliff 1 as in figure 4.13. To get possession of the first climbing rope, a group member may have to jump or lean. The distance between the first rope and cliff 1 determines how hard it is to grab the first rope.

The first group member swings from rope 1 to rope 2 and then swings rope 1 back to waiting group members on cliff 1. Teammates need to assist each other as they reach the second cliff. See figure 4.14. Group members may need to support cliff 2 so that it does not tip over or come apart. Group members can stand on the tires so that teammates swinging onto cliff 2 have plenty

Figure 4.13 Tarzan of the jungle starting position.

Figure 4.14 Tarzan of the jungle challenge.

of room to land. Group members need to plan how to help one another, how to support cliff 2 when they get there, how to pass ropes to one another, and how to balance so they do not fall off a cliff.

Conclusion of the Task

When the task is complete, all group members are standing on cliff 2 (once again, cheering as in figure 4.15).

Figure 4.15 Tarzan of the jungle success.

Additions and Variations

If you have just two climbing ropes, go ahead and try the challenge. Fewer than three ropes simplifies the task and makes it easier. If the ropes are far apart or if you want to lessen difficulty for younger students, place some extra tires in the open spaces for the group members to land on briefly. You could limit the number of teammates who may stand on these tires at one time, but you may find that these extra tires allow groups to work more closely in helping one another succeed. The size of the tires can be a separate modification. Smaller tires (such as boat trailer tires) can be more difficult to balance on than larger ones.

If your ropes are not knotted at the bottom, it is more difficult for students to hang on to them. To modify this problem, add one or two tires to the floor area to allow participants a resting or balancing spot.

Be aware of safety. Prevent group members from swinging into a wall or falling off a cliff. Also, as a group member swings onto a cliff, teammates need to avoid getting knocked off the cliff. As group members swing from rope to rope, they should concentrate on gripping the rope tightly so they do not fall onto the floor.

The Wall II

"You may be a tiller of the soil or toiler by the day; Remember, then, he does the best, the best in every way; Who has a single aim in view determined from the start; In everything he may pursue to truly do his part."

From the poem "Do Your Part," Anonymous

The Wall II is much like a sequel to a good movie or theater performance. Wall II takes the additions and variations of Wall I (Chapter 3) and makes them integral parts of this challenge. Wall II is more difficult than Wall I, and it is designed to be more challenging for older students. This task is only moderately difficult for students over sixth grade. As with Wall I, Wall II allows students to climb, an activity that elicits lots of excitement and enjoyment.

Description

The group must plan how to get everyone over the wall, especially large teammates and the last person. This wall should be higher and wider than Wall I, yet it needs to be constructed safely. Safety also requires complete cooperation from all teammates.

Success Criteria

The challenge is mastered when the group has crossed the wall. Group members must remain on mats during the challenge except when climbing the wall.

Equipment

You'll need three large crash pads or a double stack of tumbling mats 6 to 7 feet high. Two more tumbling mats (unfolded) are placed under the crash pads. See figure 4.16. A tape line divides the working area into two equal spaces.

Figure 4.16 The wall II equipment.

Setup

A 15-foot by 15-foot space should be enough for this challenge. First, lay two unfolded tumbling mats on the floor side by side (not end to end). Then, center the crash pads on the floor mats and stack the pads atop each other. If crash pads are not available, stack folded tumbling mats in a double-wide, horizontal column. Stack the mats as stably as possible by alternating the direction of each layer. Secure the stack with strapping material or jump ropes. Don't set up this challenge close to a wall or other structure.

Rules and Sacrifices

Because Wall II is not the same as Wall I, make sure the group members study the rules, understand the differences, and follow them carefully.

1. Students may not grasp crash pad handles or strapping material holding the wall together. (The face of the wall is to be treated as though it were solid.)
2. Students may not step over the line that divides the working area.
3. Once group members get down from the wall, they may not climb back up to help their teammates.
4. All group members must remain on the floor mats at all times when not on the wall and must not touch the floor next to the mats.
5. If any rule is broken, the person making the mistake and one person who has crossed the wall must start over.
6. No last names or put-downs are allowed.

Possible Solutions

It is common to see students jump and try to grasp the top of the wall by themselves. Instead, the group needs to plan how to get each other atop the wall, one by one. Because group members must remain on mats during this task, they cannot take a running start. Several ways exist to boost the first person up to reach the top of the wall (see figure 4.17), but without proper communication, the first person quite often continues over the wall to the floor below. Remember that in Wall II once group members get off the wall they cannot climb back up to help their teammates.

Watch the students as they help each other climb to the top of the wall. If too many are on top of the wall, the wall could become top-heavy and perhaps tilt or even tip over. You may want to stipulate how many group members can be on top of the wall at a time.

The group also needs a plan to help one another get off the wall safely. Because getting the last person over the wall can be the most difficult task, someone needs to stay on top of the wall to help lift this person. That person or others on top of the wall also need support from other group members. To reemphasize safety, consider a rule requiring all group members to have another's help when getting down from the wall.

Also remind group members they should not pull on teammates' clothing while assisting them; clothing could be damaged, which could be embarrassing for a group member.

Figure 4.17 The wall II challenge moving up.

Conclusion of the Task

When this challenge is mastered, group members are across the wall and are standing on the opposite side on floor mats. See figure 4.18.

Figure 4.18 Completing the wall II challenge.

Additions and Variations

You could require each team member to carry something over the wall—carry, not throw or hand it over. For instance, we have used a cone, a basketball, and a football dummy.

The Wild River

Everyone should learn that our society is not individualistic, but that most achievement is through teamwork.

Anonymous

The Wild River is unique. It requires team intelligence, team communication, team support, and team athletic prowess. This is another crossing challenge. The team must cross Wild River by planning its route around obstacles in the river.

Description

Rings and bases should be set out the length of the gym so that the colors, which denote what body part they will support, are interspersed across the river. The instructor needs to make the river crossing difficult but not impossible. Along the way, cones could be placed as obstacles to both confuse and deter the team. You also can use a balance beam as a fallen log, which students may go over or under but may not stand upon. See figure 4.19. Other obstacles in the river would be fine. Place rings and bases so team members cannot cross the river without assisting each other.

Figure 4.19 The wild river challenge.

Success Criteria

The team starts behind one end line of the gym and attempts to cross the river without falling in. The team is successful when all members cross the gym and are behind the other end line.

Equipment

All you need is a set of Olympet rings and a few indoor bases. If you do not have rings, substitute color-coded hoops or rope circles. It's fine to add balance beams or cones if you want more obstacles in the river.

Setup

The creative setup of this challenge is limited only by the teacher's imagination. The teacher must place the rings so they form a steppingstone-like path across the river. Make the path difficult by using the following criteria:

1. A blue ring can take the weight of one or more people. It is a safe ring.
2. A red ring is dangerous. No one can stand inside this ring. Red means danger!
3. An indoor base supports only one foot; no other body part can touch this base. Only one person at a time can be on a base.
4. A yellow ring supports only two hands, either two hands from one person or one hand from each of two people.
5. A white ring supports only one hand; no other body part can touch inside this ring.

Rules and Sacrifices

1. The team must remember which color ring supports which body part. If anyone enters a ring incorrectly, that person must start over.
2. Any team member who touches the floor outside a ring has fallen into the river and must start over.
3. Anyone who uses a team member's last name, negative pressure, or a put-down must start over.

Possible Solutions

The solution to this task is simple. The team must go slow, communicate, pick the best route, and help each other. One or two people should be appointed to watch out for color coding of rings and bases in case other teammates forget.

Conclusion of the Task

The river is tamed when everyone has crossed safely and correctly and is behind the end line of the gym.

Additions and Variations

Here are some of our favorite additions and variations:

- Time the crossing. Challenge the team to make it before a storm comes in 10 minutes.
- Add balance beams (fallen logs) and cones as obstacles.
- Add a climbing rope so the team must swing from one rock to another. Make sure you place a mat under the rope.
- Make the students stretch and put their body weight on their hands. Be creative!

Chapter 5

Advanced Challenges

*Success is not measured by whether
you win or whether you fail—
There's always a little bit of success,
even if things don't go your way—*

*What's important is that you'll
feel better about yourself
for the simple reason
that you tried.*

Amanda Pierce

The Black Hole

T *ogether*

E *ach*

A *ccomplishes*

M *ore*

Anonymous

The Black Hole is not only physically and intellectually challenging, but the elements of trust and cooperation are essential to developing the task. Group members will try to pass through a hula hoop suspended between two volleyball net standards. Students cannot touch the hoop (known as the Black Hole) nor can they dive through. The challenge is designed so that group members *must* help each other. This challenge is difficult and requires group members to offer lots of physical support. If groups have not worked together before, they may not have developed sufficient team-building skills to master this challenge.

Description

Group members begin on one side of the hula hoop and must remain on the tumbling mats during the challenge. Group members are to pass through the hoop to the other side and need help from teammates.

Success Criteria

The challenge is mastered when all group members have moved from the "outer space" side of the hoop (known as the Black Hole) to the "Earth" side.

Equipment

You'll need two volleyball net standards, one hula hoop, a rope to suspend the hoop between the standards, and at least four tumbling mats. See figure 5.1.

Setup

Secure the two volleyball net standards so they cannot tip or fall over during the challenge. Suspend the hula hoop between the volleyball net standards so that the bottom of the hoop is approximately 3 feet off the floor. You may need to modify the height of the hoop to accommodate shorter students; setting the hoop height so that the bottom is about waist high on the majority of your students should be sufficient.

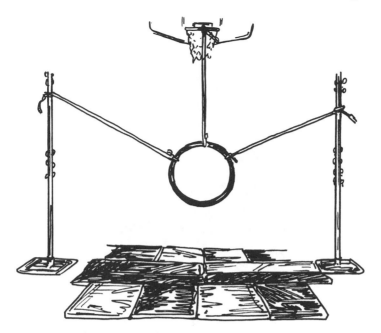

Figure 5.1 The black hole equipment.

Next, place at least four tumbling mats in the working space, at least two on each side of the hoop. A tape line may be used to help divide the working area into two distinct spaces, much like the center line of a volleyball court. Provide enough cushion in the working space so that a group member who falls will be well protected.

Rules and Sacrifices

1. All group members must go through the Black Hole.
2. No person may touch the Black Hole (hoop).
3. No one may dive through the hoop.
4. Group members must remain on tumbling mats during the challenge.
5. If any rule is broken, the person making the mistake and one person who has passed through the hoop must start again.
6. No last names or put-downs can be used.

Possible Solutions

Most groups start by lifting and sliding one group member through the hoop while keeping his or her body straight. See figure 5.2. After the first person passes through the hoop, there will be persons on both sides of the Black Hole to help their teammates through the hoop. Getting the last person through

Figure 5.2 The black hole challenge.

the hoop presents the greatest difficulty. Teammates on the Earth side of the Black Hole may reach across to the outer space side as long as they do not touch the hoop or the floor on the outer space side.

Conclusion of the Task

At the conclusion of the task, all group members are standing on the Earth side of the Black Hole and must remain on the mats until the teacher gives them approval.

Additions and Variations

Here are a few additions and variations to this challenge:

- The height of the hoop can be lowered for younger children and raised for more mature groups.
- Assigning group members to bring back "moon souvenirs" may add difficulty and interest to the task. Group members would have to carry different objects (a football, basketball, beachball, floor hockey stick, etc.) with them to Earth. The object must remain in contact with the person carrying it. Students should not pass the items to one another through the hoop.
- A time limit (15 or 20 minutes) could be established for the challenge. You could use descriptive story lines to enhance the task for younger groups ("Darth Vader will be here in 15 minutes . . .").

As we said before, this challenge involves trust and cooperation. Because no one can succeed without teammates' help, this task is good to use after the group has attempted introductory challenges.

Use enough mats so that the working space is well cushioned and safe. Group members should be lifted and moved carefully. If group members fall on the hoop, the hoop could break. (However, better to lose a hoop than have a student get injured.)

The Electric Fence

One person can be a crucial ingredient on a team but one person cannot make a team.

Kareem Abdul-Jabbar
From "The Edge" by Howard Ferguson

The Electric Fence is a favorite challenge of all age groups and can easily be modified for your students. This task requires a group to progress from one end of a high balance beam to the other end. The catch is that group members must go *under* a net (Electric Fence) hanging perpendicularly above and touching the beam. But the students can't touch the net. Even when modified this is one of the more physically challenging tasks in this book.

Description

All group members must crawl, slide, or hang like monkeys as they move from an entry mat (at one end of the beam) to an exit mat (at the other end). The group also must cross under the Electric Fence (a net hung above the beam).

Success Criteria

The task is mastered when all group members successfully cross under the fence and are standing on the exit mat.

Equipment

You'll need a high balance beam, at least seven tumbling mats, a badminton or volleyball net, and two badminton or volleyball net standards. See figure 5.3.

Setup

Place two mats end to end on the floor and set the balance beam on them. The beam should be high enough so that the tallest student cannot touch the

Figure 5.3 The electric fence equipment.

floor when hanging under the beam. Put additional mats under the beam to cover its legs and their extensions. Next, set a folded tumbling mat at each end of and perpendicular to the beam to serve as entry and exit mats. (These mats may also be called the ledges.) Place the net so that it bisects the beam. The net should hang from the standards so that it brushes the top of the beam. Cover all floor space beneath the working area with tumbling mats.

To complete this challenge, students hang under the beam and move like monkeys. As you can see from figure 5.5, group members on the entry mat (ledge 1) are supporting a guider on the beam. Group members on the exit mat (ledge 2) are helping a guider on the other side of the beam. This challenge is difficult, and the group may need several attempts to succeed.

Rules and Sacrifices

1. The students must begin the task by getting on top of the balance beam.
2. The students may not touch the floor or tumbling mats between the entry and exit mats (ledges 1 and 2).
3. Group members must go under the net without touching it.
4. The students must get back on the topside of the beam before getting off the beam.
5. Once a student gets off the beam and onto the exit mat, he or she may not get back onto the beam.
6. Only people on the beam may help group members hanging under the beam.
7. Any broken rule requires the person making the mistake and one who has crossed the beam to start over.

8. If anyone calls a person in the group by their last name or uses a put-down, the person making the mistake and one who has crossed the beam must start over.

Possible Solutions

Students climb onto the beam one at a time, turn upside down, monkey style, and try to move along the beam and under the net. While a group member tries to go under the beam and under the net, group members on both sides of the net should offer help. See figure 5.4. Most students need help getting their feet under the Electric Fence and getting back on top of the beam. Group members need to decide when to get off the beam (refer to rule 5) because if they get off the beam too soon, they may not be available to help their teammates. Constant encouragement and physical assistance are necessary during this challenge. Choosing the first and last persons to travel the beam also is vital to solving the challenge.

Figure 5.4 The electric fence challenge.

Conclusion of the Task

When their goal is reached, all group members have crossed under the Electric Fence and are standing on the exit mat (ledge 2). See figure 5.5. After you approve their success, have the group sit down at the exit mat so the recorder and summarizer can state the group's accomplishments. Group members should spend time using positive reinforcers to recognize the encouragement and praise that took place.

Additions and Variations

We have found the following variations to work well:

• Place a tire on the floor for the students to use as a support.

Figure 5.5 The electric fence success.

- Reduce travel distance for younger students and then let them drop off carefully.
- Use a lightweight football dummy as an additional group member. The students can pretend it is an injured group member being rescued.
- Assign a time limit. (Example: "A storm is coming. You have 20 minutes to complete this task.")

The Grand Canyon

Small deeds done are better than great deeds planned.
Peter Marshall, pastor, New York Avenue
Presbyterian Church, Washington, D.C.

The Grand Canyon challenges a class to work together to successfully swing by rope across an imaginary canyon. Most groups find this a favorite task; there is something exceptionally attractive to students about swinging on a rope. As with all team-building tasks or challenges, for individuals to succeed, the entire group must master the task.

Description

All group members move from a ground-level starting point (one canyon rim) to the top of a vaulting box (the other canyon rim). The distance between canyon rims is the Grand Canyon. Group members cross the canyon swinging on a rope.

Success Criteria

The task is mastered when all group members have crossed the Grand Canyon and are standing on the opposite canyon rim.

Equipment

You'll need a climbing rope, a vaulting box (or four folded tumbling mats stacked upon one another), and four to six tumbling mats placed on the floor for safety. See figure 5.6.

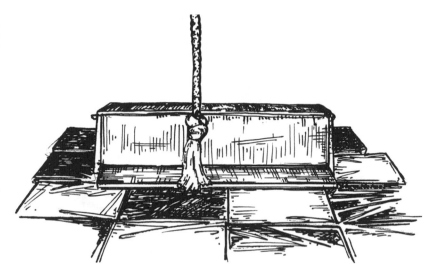

Figure 5.6 Grand Canyon equipment.

Setup

The distance between the starting line, climbing rope, and vaulting box depends on your group's ages and abilities. You may need to experiment by swinging across the canyon yourself or by letting students experiment. Place the canyon rims far enough apart to make group members work together.

For example, place a 15-foot-long tape line about 8 feet from the climbing rope to represent the beginning canyon rim. Place tumbling mats over all of the floor area where students might swing while using the rope. Place a vaulting box (or stack of mats) 6 to 8 feet on the other side of the climbing rope (14 to 16 feet from the starting line). If a vaulting box is used, put an unfolded tumbling mat over the box so that it covers the top, front, and back of the box. Remember that the distance between the canyons must be far enough to make the task somewhat difficult yet be safe. If the rope is close to a wall, place a crash pad against the wall to prevent injury.

The students swing over the Grand Canyon and onto the vaulting box as shown in figure 5.7. The group needs to help one another get onto both the rope and the vaulting box. For safety's sake, students should not crash into the vaulting box.

Figure 5.7 Starting the Grand Canyon challenge.

Rules and Sacrifices

1. The Grand Canyon is the area between the starting line and the vaulting box.
2. If any member of the group touches the floor anywhere in the Grand Canyon, a student who has successfully crossed the canyon and the person who touched the floor must start over.
3. If a group member falls or jumps off the vaulting box, that person and one other person must start over.
4. Group members must call teammates by first names only or face a sacrifice.

Stepping over the starting line violates rule 2; strictly enforce this rule.

Possible Solutions

Group members swing over the canyon, one at a time. The group should recognize that its best swingers should go first and last. The group also should recognize that if it has trouble getting a particular person across, the next person should be one who can easily cross the canyon. In the event of a sacrifice, the group will become discouraged if it has to bring back members who had trouble crossing the canyon. Therefore, the group should send back its best swingers in the event of a sacrifice.

As we suggested before, the distance between canyon rims should be enough to require the group to plan how to help each other. The swinger—grasping the rope about shoulder height—needs a push from teammates to swing across the canyon. If the swinger does not make it across, he or she either swings back to the start or slides down the rope to the floor. A swinger who successfully crosses the canyon assists other swingers onto the vaulting box. See figure 5.8. As more group members successfully cross the canyon, the helpers should support one another so that no one falls off that canyon rim. Careless swinging or other unsafe behavior cannot be allowed.

The excitement of the challenge can cause the group members to forget important strategy. It is quite common for group members to jump off the vaulting box in anticipation of a required sacrifice. If group members step off the vaulting box, an appropriate sacrifice is required; they cannot just step back onto the vaulting box.

Figure 5.8 Helping support teammates.

Conclusion of the Task

When the task is concluded, all group members are standing on the vaulting box (cheering and happy, of course) as shown in figure 5.9. After you approve their success, have them listen as the recorder and summarizer recognize the encouragement and praise that took place during the task.

Additions and Variations

You may find a student who absolutely cannot swing across on the rope. Designate a student to swing in place of the nonswinger, who nonetheless becomes a helper on the vaulting box.

Figure 5.9 Grand Canyon success.

Other variations:

- Use a football blocking dummy to represent an injured group member who needs to be rescued.
- Eliminate the vaulting box for very young children and use a folded tumbling mat.
- Use a time limit for completing the task.
- Have group members begin the challenge by standing on a folded tumbling mat and grasp the rope higher than if standing on the floor.

The Power Line

No noble thing can be done without risks.
French writer Michel de Montaigne

The Power Line is a daring task that requires group members to assume a good deal of risk. This challenge may be better suited to an athletic team than to physical education students. The Power Line is among the most advanced challenges. The challenge requires group members to be heavily involved in physically helping one another. Do not attempt this challenge unless you have a complete understanding of necessary safety precautions.

Description

Group members try to cross over a horizontal bar (usually half of even or uneven parallel bars) while standing on a board lifted by group members.

In the example we describe, group members cannot touch the bar (Power Line) with any part of their bodies, nor let the board touch the Power Line. Refer to the Additions and Variations section for ways to simplify this task and make it less risky.

The group needs to decide how to use the board and to plan the order in which group members cross the Power Line.

In this task, safety is of absolute importance. Stress safety as a rule. Group members should land feet first when going over the Power Line and should not dive or flip over the bar.

This challenge requires risk taking. Group members must be able to depend on one another for help as shown in figure 5.10. If group members haven't learned to trust each other, do not attempt this challenge.

Figure 5.10 Assisting teammates.

Success Criteria

The challenge is mastered when the entire group has been lifted over the Power Line without touching the bar with the board or with any part of a group member's body.

Equipment

You'll need a horizontal bar set not higher than the tallest group member. The bar can be half of an even or uneven parallel bar system or a rope strung between two standards. A vinyl high-jump bar is a safe substitute for a horizontal bar. You also need tumbling mats on the floor for safety. Use a large (or thick) crash pad in the landing area. You'll need an 8-foot two-by-four board. See figure 5.11.

Figure 5.11 Power line equipment.

Setup

Place six to eight mats throughout the challenge area. Set the horizontal bar equipment on the mats and cover base supports with other mats. Set the crash pad on the landing side of the Power Line. Place a tape line on the mats, if needed, to divide the working area into two parts (beginning side and ending side). Place the board on the starting side of the Power Line.

Rules and Sacrifices

1. No group member may touch the Power Line.
2. The board may not touch the Power Line.
3. Group members who have crossed the Power Line may not touch the floor on the beginning side of the Power Line nor reach under the bar to assist a teammate.
4. All group members must remain on the floor mats except when going over the Power Line.
5. If any rule is broken, the person making the mistake and one who has crossed the bar must return to the starting line.
6. No last names or put-downs can be used.

Possible Solutions

All group members must cross from one side of the Power Line to the other. Most teammates jump from a board upon which they are standing over the Power Line and land safely on a crash pad. The board can be used as an elevator to lift teammates (see figure 5.12) or be raised at an incline to allow teammates to walk the plank over the Power Line. As more group members cross the Power Line, the group may need to alter how it uses the board. The board may not cross under the Power Line and may be used only on the beginning side.

Getting the last person over the Power Line can be the greatest challenge. Some groups keep the lightest person or the person with the best gymnastic

Figure 5.12 Using the board as an elevator.

skills for last. The last person usually climbs the board as one climbs a pole. Other group members need to hold the board in a vertical or diagonal position by reaching over the Power Line to support the board. Others may reach over the Power Line to assist climbers. Remember, the board may not touch the Power Line.

Because this challenge involves more risk than other challenges, the teacher may wish to act as spotter for at least the first crosser. Then, as group members successfully cross the bar, they can help teammates land safely. Teammates may assist from both sides of the Power Line as shown in figure 5.13.

Figure 5.13 Teammates can reach over the power line.

Conclusion of the Task

When this difficult challenge is concluded, all group members are across the Power Line and are standing on a crash pad.

Additions and Variations

You could allow the board to touch the Power Line, allow a group member to place a hand on the Power Line to pull over the bar, and lower the Power Line to simplify the challenge. We do not recommend setting a time limit on this challenge because it could compromise safety.

Stepping Stones II

People acting together as a group can accomplish things which no individual acting alone could ever hope to bring about.

Franklin Delano Roosevelt
From "The Edge" by Howard Ferguson

Stepping Stones II is a real ''brain buster'' that requires much thinking and communication. It is the most difficult thinking task encountered in this book. This challenge does not require the group to work hard physically; it is more a human chess game. Cooperation and planning are essential to solving the task.

You may want to use this challenge after students have completed several other challenges or to assign it to groups demonstrating exceptional team-building skills. Refer to the Additions and Variations section for ideas on simplifying this challenge for younger students and others.

Description

The group tries to rearrange itself from a specific starting order to a specific ending order. Group members stand in a straight line on bases, which should not be moved. The team divides itself into two equal groups, and the groups face each other. See figure 5.14. There needs to be an even number of participants.

Figure 5.14 Beginning the stepping stones II challenge.

Success Criteria

The challenge is mastered when the group has moved from its beginning order to its assigned final positions.

Example: Eight students using nine bases.

Starting order:
A   B   C   D - 1   2   3   4

Ending order:
1   2   3   4 - A   B   C   D

Equipment

You need one base per group member and one extra base. (Remember: You need an even number of group members.) We use eight group members in our example, which means we need nine bases.

Setup

A space 5 to 8 feet wide and about 20 feet long will be adequate. Place the bases in a straight line, about 18 inches apart. One group member stands on each base with an empty base in the middle of the line.

The team is divided into two groups. Each teammate gets a letter or number to designate starting position. Or give teams colored jerseys to help identify their section.

Rules and Sacrifices

1.   Each group member must remain on a base except when moving to another base.
2.   A person may only move forward to another base.
3.   There may be only one person on each base at a time.
4.   When moving to a new base, a group member may move forward one base or around one teammate to another base. But team members may not move around two teammates in one move.
5.   Only one group member may move at a time.
6.   If a rule is broken or if a group cannot make another move, the group must go back to its starting order.
7.   No last names or put-downs may be used.

Possible Solutions

The solution to this challenge is so specific that you might want to practice it by making your own board game. Draw nine squares on construction paper,

| A | B | C | D | ☐ | 1 | 2 | 3 | 4 |

Figure 5.15 Solving the stepping stones II challenge.

number and letter eight checkers or domino pieces (as in figure 5.15), and practice these moves:

Step 1   D moves forward to empty base.

Step 2   1 moves around D to empty base.

Step 3   2 moves forward to empty base.

Step 4   D moves around 2 to open base.

Step 5   C moves around 1.

Step 6   B moves forward to open base.

Step 7   1 moves around B.

Step 8   2 moves around C.

Step 9   3 moves around D.

Step 10   4 moves forward to open base.

Step 11   D moves around 4 (D completes switch).

Step 12   C moves around 3.

Step 13   B moves around 2.

Step 14   A moves around 1.

Step 15   1 moves forward (1 finishes).

Step 16   2 moves around A (2 finishes).

Step 17   3 moves around B.

Step 18   4 moves around C.

Step 19   C moves forward (C finishes).

Step 20   B moves around 4 (B finishes).

Step 21   A moves around 3.

Step 22   3 moves forward (3 finishes).

Step 23   4 moves around A (4 finishes).

Step 24   A moves forward (the task is complete). See figure 5.16.

Whew! Got that? See why we called it a human chess game? The group needs to communicate constantly with one another.

Figure 5.16 Stepping stones II success.

Conclusion of the Task

The challenge is mastered when group members have moved from their beginning order to the designated ending order. As mentioned before, to prevent great frustration group members may need to practice the challenge as a board game before trying it as a physical challenge.

Additions and Variations

Have group members start practicing in a four-person group (this takes eight moves) or in a six-person group (this takes 15 moves).

This is a very difficult challenge and should not be tried with groups that had trouble with easier tasks. Make modifications that we have overlooked. Keep in mind that this challenge requires more mental gymnastics and communication than physical skill. When groups master this challenge they should be considered good, cooperative problem solvers.

To give your group visual help, tape a letter or number to each member's jersey. One group could wear red jerseys with letters A, B, C, and D. The other group could wear blue jerseys with the numbers 1, 2, 3, and 4.

Jungle Trail

We have worked hard, accomplished much, and had fun doing it. We did these things because we have team pride.

Glover & Midura

Description

This is a real "Raiders of the Lost Ark" challenge. It can be the culminating challenge in your class, but it is one students will want to do again and again.

They will love it! After you start Jungle Trail you will amaze yourself with the number of creative ideas that pop into your head.

The setup for this task is involved, so try to leave the equipment in place for at least two days. This challenge combines several of the challenges we've already presented to create a series of challenges. Equipment needs are similar to earlier challenges.

Equipment

You'll need equipment used in these challenges:

Power Line: Uneven parallel bar, two-by-four board, crash pad, and mats.

Grand Canyon: Swinging rope, crash pads, and mats.

Electric Fence: High balance beam, volleyball net and standards, and mats.

Teamwork Walk: Teamwork walking boards.

Wild River: Olympet rings, indoor bases, and cones.

You can also use extra balance beams between the challenges to make "Jungle Trail" more difficult.

Setup

Make a trail for the students to follow upon which they encounter wild rivers, electric fences, grand canyons, and other challenges you have planned along the way.

As you can see from figure 5.17, the Trail presents some challenges new to students, but most they've already worked on. Adding balance beams and two-by-four boards increases the challenge and excitement.

As you can see in figure 5.18, using a hurdle above a balance beam requires students to duck under or crawl on hands and knees to cross the beam.

A block of wood under one side of a beam makes it wobble. See figure 5.19. If you add a bowling pin on the wobbly side, the pin falls easily unless the child walking the beam is careful.

Success Criteria

The success criteria for this challenge are like other challenges. The team must travel through Jungle Trail without touching the floor and must achieve the success criteria on each challenge along the way. (These success criteria were covered in previous sections.) The only new areas are the balance beams. Swinging ropes must not touch any team member crossing the beam.

Start each team on a separate challenge and let it travel along the trail at its own speed, perhaps even in different directions. This way teams may meet in the middle of a challenge or in the middle of a balance beam. Teamwork within and between teams is crucial.

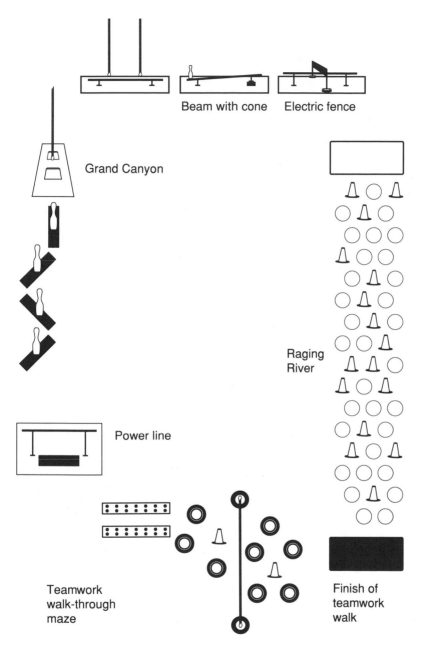

Beam with cone   **Electric fence**

Grand Canyon

Raging River

Power line

Teamwork walk-through maze

Finish of teamwork walk

Figure 5.17   The jungle trail challenge.

Set up this trail as creatively as possible. For younger children, remove some obstacles and add more appropriate ones. When you set up, keep in mind that you want teammates to start and finish the Jungle Trail as a team, so make sure obstacles require team effort.

Figure 5.18 Balance beam through a hurdle.

Figure 5.19 Unstable balance beam with bowling pin.

Possible Solutions

Solving Jungle Trail is easy if students take their time and work as a team.

Conclusion of the Task

When the team completes the Jungle Trail and arrives back at its starting point, it has completed the challenge.

Additions and Variations

Be creative and add your own variations to Jungle Trail.

Rules and Sacrifices

1. If anyone touches the floor at any time, that person must start that challenge over. Do not use sacrifices on Jungle Trail.
2. All rules outlined previously for the challenges are in effect.
3. Every team member must use at least one Praise Phrase during the journey.
4. No last names, put-downs, or negative pressure are allowed. Anyone breaking this rule must start over at the point of the mistake.

This challenge can culminate the team-building unit. By conquering all the challenges and new obstacles along the way, the team builds a closeness. A real feeling of TEAM develops. We encourage you to take the time and invest the creativity necessary to teach this team-building challenge.

Appendix

TEAM REPORT CARD

1. How did our team involve everyone in solving the challenge?

2. Did our team use negative pressure or put-downs during the challenge?

3. Did we listen to one another and use ideas that we shared?

4. How many and which team members used Praise Phrases or positive encouragement?

5. What were some of the Praise Phrases used?

INSTRUCTOR PREPARATION FORM

Challenge: _____

Level of Difficulty:

Equipment Needed:

To Master the Challenge:

Rules and Sacrifices:

Variations:

Safety Considerations:

Alphabet Balance Beam

Equipment
A high balance beam, plenty of tumbling mats for safety, and two crash pads.

Starting Position
Group members sit on the balance beam in random order. The teacher may assign the group to arrange itself alphabetically by first name, middle name, last name, etc.

Our Challenge
The task is completed when all members are standing on the beam in the assigned alphabetical order.

Rules and Sacrifices
1. All group members must stay on the beam during the task.
2. If any person touches the mats or legs of the beam, the entire team must resume its starting position and start over.
3. No last names or put-downs are allowed.

Starting Position   Finish Position
(example): First names

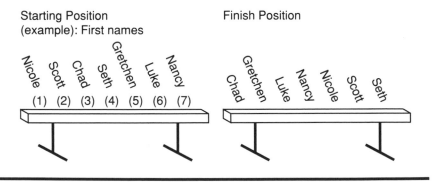

Alphabet Balance Beam

Questions

1. By which names are we alphabetizing ourselves?
2. In which direction are we alphabetizing?
3. What happens if a person touches the floor during the task?
4. What happens if a person touches the support legs of the beam?
5. What will we be doing when we have completed the challenge?

CHALLENGE CARD   River Crossing

Equipment
Two scooters, at least one long jump rope, and two deck tennis rings.

Starting Position
All group members start on one side of the river. Place all equipment there.

Our Challenge
The task is completed when all group members have crossed without touching the river with any part of their bodies. All equipment also must be brought across the river.

Rules and Sacrifices
1. The river is the area between the end line and midcourt line of the basketball court.
2. If any part of a person's body touches the river (the floor), that person and another who has crossed the river must start over.
3. If a person enters the river to retrieve equipment, one successful crosser must be sacrificed.
4. The first person across the river cannot be sacrificed during the task.
5. No one should use last names or put-downs.

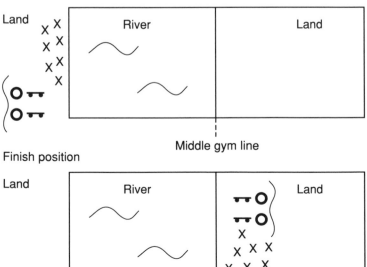

Questions

1. What equipment will we use?
2. Where is the river?
3. What happens if a person touches the river?
4. Who cannot be sacrificed?
5. How will we know the challenge is completed?
6. Where does the equipment have to be at the end of the task?

The Rock

Equipment

One tumbling mat and one 13-inch tire.

Starting Position

Group members stand on the tumbling mat next to the rock.

Our Challenge

The task is completed when all group members are balanced on the rock (off the floor) for a slow count of "one-and-two-and-three-and-four-and-five."

Rules and Sacrifices

1. All group members must be off the floor.
2. Group members do not have to be touching the rock.
3. Stepping off the rock and touching the floor for even an instant means the group must start over with no one on the rock.
4. When the group is ready, get the teacher's attention to witness the attempted solution.
5. Students should not call each other by last names or use put-downs.

Questions

1. What equipment will we use?
2. What happens if someone touches the floor after being on the rock?
3. How long do we have to stay on the rock?
4. Do we all have to be touching the rock?
5. Who does the counting for our task?

CHALLENGE CARD

The Snake

Equipment
One tug-of-war rope.

Starting Position
All group members begin in the center of their assigned working space with the rope neatly curled.

Our Challenge
The group makes eight specific shapes (letters, numbers, words, etc.) using the tug-of-war rope. When the shape is made, group members must use their bodies to cover the entire rope. Shapes are either assigned by the teacher or created by the group.

Rules and Sacrifices
1. Shapes must be made by using the rope as a guide.
2. All group members must be on the rope.
3. The rope must be completely covered by group members.
4. The group must have each shape approved by the teacher before creating the next shape.
5. No one should call other people by their last names or use put-downs.

The Snake

Questions

1. What equipment do we use?
2. How many shapes do we make?
3. Who has to be on the rope?
4. What do we do with the rope?
5. What do we do after the teacher approves the shape?

Equipment
One base for each group member and one extra base.

Starting Position
All group members stand on one base each, leaving an open base at one end of the line. Group members number off so each knows where to begin and end the task.

Our Challenge
The task is completed when the group is in the exact reverse order from its starting order.

Example
Starting position: 1 2 3 4 5 6 7 8
Ending position: 8 7 6 5 4 3 2 1

Rules and Sacrifices
1. Only one person may touch a base at a time.
2. A person may move in either direction to a neighboring base.
3. Group members may touch a new base only if it is empty.
4. The bases may not be moved.
5. Tennis shoes must be worn.
6. If more than one person touches a base, the entire group must start over.
7. No one should call other people by their last names or use put-downs.
8. If anyone touches the floor, the entire group must start over.

Starting Position:

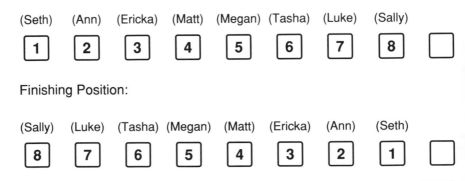

(Seth)   (Ann)   (Ericka)   (Matt)   (Megan) (Tasha)   (Luke)   (Sally)

| 1 | 2 | 3 | 4 | 5 | 6 | 7 | 8 | |

Finishing Position:

(Sally)   (Luke)   (Tasha) (Megan)   (Matt)   (Ericka)   (Ann)   (Seth)

| 8 | 7 | 6 | 5 | 4 | 3 | 2 | 1 | |

Stepping Stones I

Questions

1. What are we trying to accomplish?
2. How many bases do we get?
3. What happens if someone touches the floor?
4. What happens if more than one person touches a base at the same time?
5. What are some ways we can help each other?

CHALLENGE CARD

Teamwork Walk

Equipment
One set of team skis and a designated path.

Starting Position
Group members stand on the team skis at the starting line with their feet in the footholds.

Our Challenge
The task is completed when group members have completed the course without anyone touching the floor, a wall, or any other stationary object with any part of their bodies.

Rules and Sacrifices
1. All group members must have their feet in the footholds.
2. No one may touch the floor, wall, or other stationary part of the gymnasium with any part of his or her body.
3. Group members must travel the designated path from start to finish.
4. If a rule is broken, the group must start over.
5. No one should call other people by their last names or use put-downs.

ORGANIZER CARD   Teamwork Walk

Questions

1. Where is our starting point?
2. Where is our ending point?
3. What happens if someone touches the floor while we are walking?
4. What happens if someone touches a wall or uses another object for support while we are walking?
5. What can we do to physically support one another?

CHALLENGE CARD The Whole World in Their Hands

Equipment
One cage ball (or earth ball) 48 inches in diameter or larger.

Starting Position
The group sits crab walk style around the cage ball while the ball sits on the first tire.

Our Challenge
The task is completed when the cage ball has been moved from the first tire, across the gymnasium to the second tire without the ball touching the floor.

Rules and Sacrifices
1. The cage ball cannot touch the floor.
2. The cage ball cannot touch the hands or arms of any group member.
3. If a rule is broken, the ball is returned to tire 1 and the group starts over.
4. No one should call others by their last names or use put-downs.

ORGANIZER CARD The Whole World in Their Hands

Questions
1. What is our starting position?
2. Where do we put the cage ball?
3. What body parts cannot touch the cage ball?
4. What happens if the ball touches the floor?
5. What happens if we touch the ball with our hands or arms?

CHALLENGE CARD

The Tire Bridge

Equipment

One tire for each group member and one extra tire.

Starting Position

The group is on one side of the river with a stack of tires.

Our Challenge

The task is completed when the tire bridge has been used to move the group from one end of the gymnasium to the other end (across the river). The group must be on land with tires stacked vertically.

Rules and Sacrifices

1. Only one person may be on a tire at a time.
2. If anyone touches the river with any part of the body, the bridge must move back to the starting position.
3. If two people step on one tire at the same time, the bridge must move back to the starting position.
4. No one should call others by their last names or use put-downs.

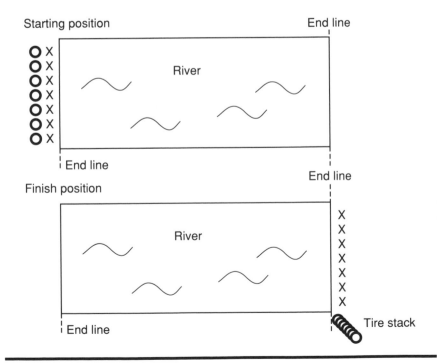

Questions

1. Where are the river boundaries?
2. How many tires do we get?
3. What happens if someone touches the river (floor)?
4. What happens if two people step on a tire at the same time?
5. Where will we be when we are done with the task?
6. What will we do with the tires when we reach land?

The Wall I

Equipment
A large crash pad or a tall stack of tumbling mats and two unfolded tumbling mats under the wall.

Starting Position
Group members are on a mat on one side of the wall.

Our Challenge
The task is completed when all group members cross the wall.

Rules and Sacrifices
1. The wall must not fall over.
2. Group members may not hold on to crash pad handles or ropes tied around the wall.
3. No one may step over the tape line dividing the tumbling mats into two sections.
4. If the wall falls over, the entire group must start over.
5. If either rule 2 or rule 3 is broken, the person making the mistake and one person already over the wall must start over.
6. No one should call other people by their last names or use put-downs.

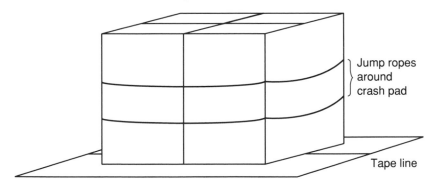

Jump ropes around crash pad

Tape line

Questions

1. What is our challenge?
2. What happens if someone steps over the tape line?
3. What happens if someone grabs the rope or mat handles?
4. What happens if the wall falls over?
5. Where will we be when the task is done?

CHALLENGE CARD   Bridge Over the Raging River

Equipment
Four tires, two long jump ropes, and two 8-foot two-by-fours.

Starting Position
All group members begin at the starting line at one end of the river with their equipment.

Our Challenge
The task is completed when all group members have crossed the river without touching the floor. They must bring along all equipment.

Rules and Sacrifices
1. Group members may not touch the river (floor).
2. Group members may not step on a two-by-four if one end of the board is in the river.
3. If a rule is broken, the group must take all equipment back to the starting line and start over.

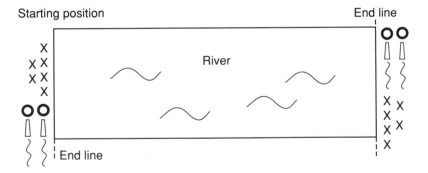

4. If the two-by-four touches the river under the weight of group members stepping on it, no sacrifice is required.
5. No one should call others by their last names or use put-downs.

Safety Note
Be careful that no one steps on the end of a two-by-four so that the board flips up.

Bridge Over the Raging River

Questions

1. What equipment will we use?
2. Where are the river boundaries?
3. What happens if a person touches the river (floor)?
4. What happens if the two-by-four is in the river and someone steps on it?
5. Where will we be when the task is completed?
6. What is the special safety note?

The Human Billboard

Equipment

A hanging cargo net, tumbling mats under the net, a list of letters to be constructed, and paper and pencils for drawing plans.

Starting Position

All group members stand on mats next to the net. All group members begin on one side of the net.

Our Challenge

Using all group members on the cargo net, the team must construct 8 out of 12 letters assigned by the teacher.

Rules and Sacrifices

1. All group members must be on the same side of the cargo net.
2. All group members must be off the floor.
3. All group members must get off the cargo net before a new letter is constructed.
4. No one should call other people by their last names or use put-downs.

There are no sacrifices. The teacher approves the constructed letter before a new one can be built.

         # The Human Billboard

Questions

1. What equipment do we use?
2. How many letters do we construct?
3. How many group members must be on the cargo net?
4. Do we have to be on the same side of the cargo net?
5. What are the sacrifices?
6. What do we do when the teacher approves a letter?

CHALLENGE CARD   Jumping Machine

Equipment
One tug-of-war rope.

Starting Position
All group members stand next to the tug-of-war rope as it lays on the floor.

Our Challenge
The task is mastered when all group members have completed 10 consecutive jumps without a miss. All jumpers must jump at the same time.

Rules and Sacrifices
1. There may be only one group member at each end of the rope. All other members must jump.
2. The 10 jumps must be consecutive. If a miss occurs, the task begins again.
3. The rope must be turned so that it goes over the heads and below the feet of group members.
4. Counting does not begin until all jumpers are jumping.
5. No one should call other people by their last names or use put-downs.

Jumping Machine

Questions

1. What equipment will we use?
2. How many jumps must we accomplish?
3. Do our jumps have to be consecutive?
4. What do we do if we miss?
5. Must the rope pass over our heads?
6. Shall we count our jumps out loud?
7. When do we start counting our jumps?

CHALLENGE CARD   Quicksand

Equipment
A cargo net, one long jump rope, and at least four tumbling mats for safety.

Starting Position
All group members stand behind the starting line on one side of the cargo net. The net hangs over the quicksand.

Our Challenge
The task is completed when all group members have crossed the quicksand and are standing on the land mat.

Rules and Sacrifices
1. The quicksand is the area between the boundary lines.
2. If any group member touches the quicksand (the floor or mats in the quicksand), that person and one person who has crossed the quicksand must go back to the starting position.
3. No one should call other people by their last names or use put-downs.
4. Keep the land mat from crossing the tape line.

Please be safe and use good judgment while swinging on the net.

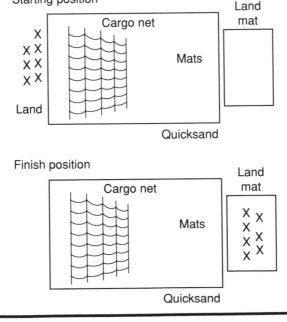

Quicksand

Questions

1. What equipment do we use?
2. Where does the quicksand exist?
3. What happens if someone touches quicksand?
4. What should we do if the land mat crosses the tape line?
5. Where will we be when the challenge is completed?

Equipment
Three or more climbing ropes, mats on the floor for safety, a vaulting box or stack of mats for cliff 1 and for cliff 2, and two or more tires.

Starting Position
All group members begin on cliff 1.

Our Challenge
All group members must swing from cliff 1 to cliff 2 using ropes. All group members are standing on cliff 2 when the task is done.

Rules and Sacrifices
1. If a person touches the floor (or mats) between cliff 1 and cliff 2, that person and one who has already swung to cliff 2 must go back to the beginning.
2. If a person falls off a cliff, he or she must return to cliff 1 along with one other person who has swung to cliff 2.
3. Group members may stand on tires to help support cliff 2 or their teammates.
4. No one should call other people by their last names or use put-downs.

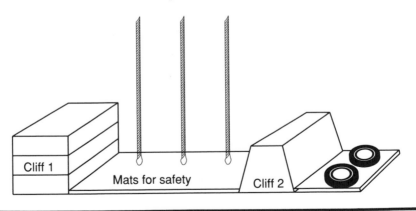

Questions

1. What equipment will we use for this challenge?
2. Where will we all start the challenge?
3. Where will we all finish the challenge?
4. What happens if someone touches the floor?
5. What happens if someone falls off a cliff?
6. How can we use the tires?

The Wall II

Equipment

Three large crash pads stacked on one another and tumbling mats under the wall.

Starting Position

All group members stand on a floor mat on one side of the wall.

Our Challenge

The task is completed when all group members cross over the wall and are standing on the mat next to the wall.

Rules and Sacrifices

1. Group members may not hold on to crash pad handles.
2. Group members may not step over the line dividing the area into two sections.
3. Once group members get off the top of the wall, they may not climb back up to help teammates.
4. Students must stay on the mats at all times when they are not on the wall. They may not touch the floor.
5. If any rule is broken, the person making the mistake and one person who has completed the challenge must start over.
6. No one should call other people by their last names or use put-downs.

The Wall II

Questions

1. What is our challenge?
2. What happens if someone steps over the tape line?
3. What happens if someone steps off the mats?
4. What happens if someone grabs the ropes or mat handles?
5. What happens if someone gets off the top of the wall?
6. Where will we be when the task is done?

CHALLENGE CARD

The Wild River

Equipment

Blue, red, yellow, and white Olympet rings, and a few indoor bases.

Starting Position

The team stands behind the end line at the start of the Wild River trail.

Our Challenge

The Wild River is mastered when everyone moves from one end of the gym to the other without going outside any rings or bases. Group members can use rings and bases only in certain ways.

A blue ring is safe. More than one person can stand in it.

A red ring is danger! No one can use it.

A yellow ring supports two hands, either both from one person or one from each of two people.

A white ring supports only one hand.

An indoor base supports only one foot.

Rules and Sacrifices

1. Anyone who touches the floor outside the rings or bases must start over.
2. Anyone who uses a ring or base incorrectly must start over.
3. No last names, negative pressure, or put-downs can be used. Start over if you use these terms.

The Wild River

Questions

1. What happens if someone touches the floor outside a ring?
2. What happens if someone uses a ring incorrectly?
3. Where is our starting point?
4. Where do we finish?
5. What happens if group members use put-downs or call people by their last names?

The Black Hole

Equipment
Two volleyball net standards, one hula hoop, jump ropes to suspend the hula hoop from volleyball standards, and at least four tumbling mats for safety.

Starting Position
All group members stand on one side of the suspended hula hoop (Black Hole). Group members must remain on tumbling mats.

Our Challenge
The task is mastered when all group members have been passed from one side of the hoop (outer space) through the hoop (Black Hole) to the other side (Earth).

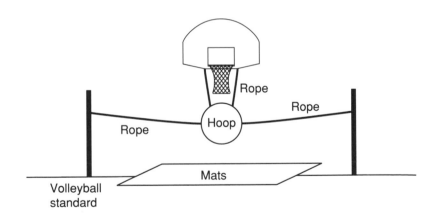

Rules and Sacrifices
1. All group members must pass through the hoop.
2. Group members may not touch the hoop.
3. No one may step over the dividing line.
4. All group members must remain on tumbling mats during the task.
5. No one should call other people by their last names or use put-downs.
6. If a rule is broken, the person making the mistake and one successful person must start over.

Questions

1. What is our starting position?
2. What is our ending position?
3. What happens if someone touches the Black Hole (hoop)?
4. What happens if someone steps over the dividing line?
5. What happens if someone dives through the hoop?

CHALLENGE CARD   The Electric Fence

Equipment

A high balance beam, tumbling mats for safety, a volleyball net, and two volleyball net standards.

Starting Position

All group members stand on the entry mat at one end of the balance beam.

Our Challenge

The task is completed when all group members have advanced from entry mat to exit mat without touching the Electric Fence (net). All group members must pass under the net.

Rules and Sacrifices

1. Group members must go under the Electric Fence (net) without touching it.
2. Group members may not touch the floor or mats between the entry and exit mats.
3. Group members must begin the task by getting on top of the balance beam.
4. Group members must get back on top of the beam before getting off the beam.
5. Once group members get off the beam and onto the exit mat, they may not get back onto the beam.
6. No one should call other people by their last names or use put-downs.
7. Any broken rule requires the person making the mistake and one who has completed the task to start over.

The Electric Fence

Questions

1. Where is the entry mat?
2. Where is the exit mat?
3. What happens if we touch the floor between the entry and exit mats?
4. Must we go under the net (fence)?
5. What happens if we touch the net?
6. What do we have to do before we get off the beam?
7. Where will we be when we finish the challenge?

Equipment

One climbing rope, one vaulting box (or vertical column of mats), tumbling mats on the floor for safety, and tape for a starting line.

Starting Position

All group members stand behind the starting line, facing the vaulting box. A tape line on the floor marks the starting line.

Our Challenge

The task is completed when all group members have crossed the Grand Canyon and are standing on the vaulting box.

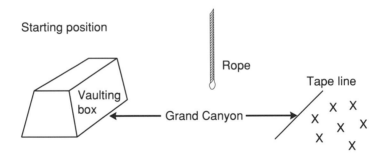

Rules and Sacrifices

1. The Grand Canyon is the area between the starting line and the vaulting box.
2. If any member of the group touches the floor anywhere in the Grand Canyon, one member of the group who has successfully crossed the canyon and the person touching the floor must start over.
3. If a group member falls off the vaulting box, that person and one successful person must start over.
4. No one should call other people by last names or use put-downs. The person making the mistake and one other successful person must start over.

The Grand Canyon

Questions

1. Where is the Grand Canyon?
2. What happens if someone touches the Grand Canyon?
3. What happens if someone falls off the vaulting box?
4. What if someone steps over the starting line?
5. What will we be doing when the challenge is completed?

CHALLENGE CARD

The Power Line

Equipment

One horizontal bar (such as half a parallel even or uneven bar set), six to eight tumbling mats, one crash pad, and one 8-foot two-by-four.

Starting Position

All group members stand on a mat on the starting side of the horizontal bar (Power Line).

Our Challenge

The task is completed when all group members have crossed over the Power Line without touching it. The board cannot touch the Power Line.

Rules and Sacrifices

1. Neither group members crossing nor others helping may touch the Power Line.
2. Group members must stay on the mats except when crossing the Power Line.
3. No one should call other people by their last names or use put-downs.
4. If a rule is broken, the person making the mistake and one who has crossed the bar must start over.

ORGANIZER CARD The Power Line

Questions

1. Where is the entry mat?
2. Where is the exit mat?
3. What happens if we touch the Power Line?
4. What happens if the board touches the Power Line?
5. May we step off entry or exit mats?
6. Where will we be when we finish the challenge?

Stepping Stones II

Equipment

Nine indoor bases or carpet squares set in a straight line. Different colored jerseys to identify the two halves of the team.

Starting Position

Each group member stands on a base with an empty base in the middle of the line. Group members get a letter or number. Example: 4 3 2 1 - A B C D
The team is split into halves and faces toward the empty base.

Our Challenge

The task is completed when the halves of the team end up like this:
A B C D - 4 3 2 1

Rules and Sacrifices

1. Only one person may move to a base at a time.
2. Team members may not move backward.
3. Only one person may be on a base at a time.
4. Group members may move to an empty base directly in front of them or go around another person to an empty base.
5. If a rule is broken, all group members must go back to their original bases.
6. No one should call other people by their last names or use put-downs.

Stepping Stones II

Questions

1. How will we line up to start this challenge?
2. How will we be lined up when we complete the challenge?
3. Where will the extra base be?
4. When can we move off our base?
5. Can we move backward?
6. Can two people move at the same time?
7. Can we move two or more bases in one move?
8. How many people may be on one base at a time?

About the Authors

Don Glover   Dan Midura

Don Glover has taught physical education, including adapted physical education, since 1967 at the preschool, elementary, secondary, and postsecondary levels. In addition, he teaches graduate classes in adapted physical education methods at St. Thomas University in St. Paul.

In 1981, Glover was recognized as Minnesota's Teacher of the Year, and in 1989 he was named the Minnesota Adapted Physical Education Teacher of the Year. He has published numerous magazine and journal articles on physical education and sport and has been a clinician at more than 50 workshops and clinics.

Glover earned his master's degree in physical education from Winona State University. He is a member of the American Alliance for Health, Physical Education, Recreation and Dance (AAHPERD), the Minnesota Association for Health, Physical Education, Recreation and Dance (MAHPERD), and the Minnesota Education Association.

Dan Midura is the elementary physical education resource teacher for the Roseville, Minnesota Area School District. He has taught physical education since 1970.

Midura received his master's degree from the University of Minnesota and was selected Outstanding Physical Education Student in 1970. He is a member of AAHPERD and MAHPERD.